PHILOSOPHY
ALL THAT MATTERS

Julian Baggini

PHILOSOPHY

Julian Baggini

ALL THAT MATTERS

ALL THAT MATTERS

Hodder Education
338 Euston Road, London NW1 3BH.

Hodder Education is an Hachette UK company

First published in UK 2012 by Hodder Education

First published in US 2012 by The McGraw-Hill Companies, Inc.

This edition published 2012

Copyright © 2012 Julian Baggini

The moral rights of the author have been asserted

Database right Hodder Education (makers)

British Library Cataloguing in Publication Data: a catalogue record for this title is available from the British Library.

Library of Congress Catalog Card Number: on file.

10 9 8 7 6 5 4

The publisher has used its best endeavours to ensure that any website addresses referred to in this book are correct and active at the time of going to press. However, the publisher and the author have no responsibility for the websites and can make no guarantee that a site will remain live or that the content will remain relevant, decent or appropriate.

The publisher has made every effort to mark as such all words which it believes to be trademarks. The publisher should also like to make it clear that the presence of a word in the book, whether marked or unmarked, in no way affects its legal status as a trademark.

Every reasonable effort has been made by the publisher to trace the copyright holders of material in this book. Any errors or omissions should be notified in writing to the publisher, who will endeavour to rectify the situation for any reprints and future editions.

Hachette UK's policy is to use papers that are natural, renewable and recyclable products and made from wood grown in sustainable forests. The logging and manufacturing processes are expected to conform to the environmental regulations of the country of origin.

www.hoddereducation.co.uk

Typeset by Cenveo Publisher Services.

Printed in Great Britain by CPI Group (UK) Ltd, Croydon, CR0 4YY.

Contents

Acknowledgements   vi

About the Author   vii

1 Why philosophy matters   1

2 In search of truth   9

3 Representing reality   25

4 Ultimate reality   39

5 Modelling the universe   55

6 Surveying the heavens   67

7 Who and what are we?   79

8 The value of art   99

9 States and nature   89

10 Doing right and doing well   109

11 The meaning of life   123

Appendix: 100 Ideas   135

Index   147

Acknowledgements

The author and publishers would like to thank the following for their permission to reproduce photos in this book. Chapter 3: © artSILENSEcom – Fotolia; Chapter 4: ©Photodisc/Getty Images; Chapter 5: © The Art Gallery Collection / Alamy; Chapter 6: © Howard Sandler – Fotolia; Chapter 7: © The Art Gallery Collection / Alamy; Chapter 8: © laurent dambies – Fotolia; Chapter 9: William Murphy/ http://www.flickr.com/photos/infomatique/5037516242/ http://creativecommons.org/licenses/by-sa/2.0; Chapter 10: © .shock – Fotolia; Chapter 11: © Stan Pritchard / Alamy.

About the Author

Julian Baggini is a writer and journalist, who was recently named on the *Observer*'s list of Britain's top public intellectuals. His doctorate was from University College London on the philosophy of personal identity, and his books have been published globally and translated into many languages around the world including Russian, Spanish and Korean.

Baggini is widely regarded as one of the most lucid and accessible writers of public philosophy. His work appears in national and international newspapers and magazines such as the *Wall Street Journal*, *FT*, *Guardian*, *Independent*, *Asia Literary Review* and *Prospect* and he co-founded *The Philosophers' Magazine*.

Julian has also made cameo appearances in two Alexander McCall Smith novels, and been the subject of a question in University Challenge.

Follow Julian at:
www.julianbaggini.com
@microphilosophy

1

Why Philosophy Matters

ALL THAT MATTERS

Although it is fashionable in some quarters to put down human beings, most of us, if honest, would agree that *Homo sapiens* is a pretty amazing species. But when it comes to explaining what makes us different from (if not better than) the other animals, people radically disagree. People often point to our ability to use language or simply to our opposable thumbs, which can allow humans to manipulate physical objects much more intricately than any other animal. But neither of these seems to capture humanity's uniqueness. Other species may lack our rich and flexible language, but they still communicate. We may be more skilled at manipulating objects, but even chimps make basic tools.

So here's another suggestion: one which explains why we're different, why philosophy lies at the heart of that difference and why philosophy matters.

▶ The first philosopher

Consider early humans. They could talk, they made clothes, built huts and so on. Already they appear quite different from other animals. But in one important respect, they are just the same. When the bird flies south for winter, the beaver builds its dam or the lion hunts its prey, it does so simply because *that is what it does*. Our early human is exactly the same. She may be a bit better at thinking about which means can be used to achieve what end, but still, like a cat, she hunts, she eats, she reproduces, she shelters, she plays and she dies because *that is what she does*.

Then, one day, a human has a thought that perhaps nothing in the entire universe has had before: *why should I do what I do?* Instead of just killing a boar and eating it, she wonders whether this is the only way to live. You can imagine how this question would have gone down around the fire. Even today, people often struggle to explain why they do what they do. Think of how many people from older generations explain why they married young with the simple, 'It was just what you did in those days'. Before our species' first philosophical moment, *everything* was just what we did in those days.

Our original philosopher has, in effect, asked what has historically been one of the central questions of philosophy: What's the point of it all? What is the meaning of life? From this question, all other philosophical questions follow, even those that appear to be quite abstract and far removed from everyday concerns.

For instance, if you ask how you should live, you are beginning to ask questions of ethics: what we *ought* to do, not just what we in fact do. There is increasing evidence that some other animals, particularly primates, are able to show compassion and have some sense of fairness and reciprocity. But although this points to some primitive ethical sense, none seems capable of reflecting on what it means to say we 'ought' to do something. This marked the third major step forward in thinking. First, primitive minds simply perceived the world through the senses, representing the world *as it is*. Second, more sophisticated minds modelled that world and used imagination to represent it *as it could be*. What was entirely new when ethics emerged is that for the first time we think not just descriptively but *normatively*: about the world *as it should be*.

It is a small step from thinking about 'How ought I to live?' to 'How ought we to live, together?', which leads us to political philosophy. Other animals have a politics of sorts. They organize themselves in social groups, have hierarchies and leaders, protocols and even implicit rules of conduct. What they do not do, however, is change these practices on the basis of reflection on the best ways to order their societies. This human ability is again of a radically unique kind, and it emerges from a basic ability to think philosophically about the normative dimension of life.

Having got this far, it would not escape our attention for long that this normative dimension extends beyond questions of how to live and that we also make value judgements about works or art, natural beauty and food and drink. We would have stumbled across another area of philosophy: aesthetics.

▶ Digging deeper

What we can see is that once that first 'why?' is asked, to answer one philosophical question, we have to dig deeper and address others that lie beneath it. And so the process continues. Thinking about how we ought to live, individually and in society, invites the question, 'What kind of creatures are we anyway?' Another area, sometimes called philosophical anthropology, has been opened up: the nature of human life.

But to understand the nature of human beings we have to understand the nature of the universe we live in, and that leads us to metaphysics, and also to the question of whether or not anything is in charge of it all – and so to the philosophy of religion. Still the questions get deeper. On what do we base our understanding of the universe? Above all, on science. But what exactly is that, and how does it work? We need a philosophy of science to find out.

Even science does not lie at the very base of our understanding. To do science, we first have to represent the world, in language and in perception. In a strange way, this brings us back full circle to where philosophy began. First we represented the world, then we questioned the world and finally we questioned our representation of the world.

The journey represents philosophy's growth from birth to maturity, and it is in that maturity that some of the most difficult and abstract-seeming questions emerge: What is knowledge? What is truth? Can we ever obtain either? This take us into very deep waters. Consider, for instance, the question of whether philosophical problems have been discovered or invented. There is a sense in which they did not exist until people started to think about them. But the way I have told the story, it seems that, in another sense, these questions and issues were always there: they simply required human beings to stumble across them. So is philosophy itself a human construction or does it have some real existence of its own? This question shows philosophy's distinctive need to constantly reflect upon itself and so to add layer on layer of reflection. If philosophy became an adult when it questioned our representation of the world, perhaps it only became fully mature when it became capable of questioning its own questioning.

This development of enquiry, from the first 'why?' to the most complex questions of abstract theory of knowledge, is not supposed to be an historical hypothesis about what actually happened. Rather, it is a fable, one which both suggests what really makes humans different and shows how the questions of philosophy relate. As such, it also in part explains why people have different views about what the most basic question in philosophy is. In one way, it is the question of how to live, as it is that which (often, if not always) provides the basic motivation to ask all the other questions. But in other ways, the most basic questions are the ones we come to last, as it is those that have to be answered first if we are to put all the pieces of the jigsaw together so that we can finally work out what the point of life is.

So, in this book I'm going to address the questions in what, in my fable, is reverse chronological order. Rather than start with the concrete and drift off into the abstract, we will start with what seems abstract and show how that feeds into the most important existential questions of all. Of course, once we ask abstract questions, they can take on their own life, and many people pursue them for no other reason than that their human curiosity finds in them intriguing puzzles to be solved. There is nothing wrong with this. Philosophers are no more under an obligation to always think of the practical than mathematicians or scientists. But I want to show that these questions are not just interesting for their own sake. Living the examined life requires at least some engagement with questions around what we can know and how we can know it.

2

In Search of Truth

Does acupuncture work and, if so, to what degree and for what conditions? Can our planet sustain its current population or are we already over capacity? Which school is best for my child? Do I need to lose weight? Did Lee Harvey Oswald really act alone?

From the mundane to the metaphysical, it is the human condition to wonder about what is true and what we can know. For the most part, however, we ponder whether particular things are true or false, known or unknown, without taking a further step back and asking ourselves what 'truth' and 'knowledge' actually mean. For most practical purposes, we don't need to. If I say I know what time your bus leaves, or that someone important has just died, you don't need to have studied philosophy to understand what I mean. For you to say, 'But what do you mean by "know"?' would be inappropriate and unhelpfully picky.

Why, then, might we nonetheless think that is a good question, worth trying to answer? Tellingly, this is itself a philosophical question. However we define philosophy – and it is notoriously difficult to come up with a definition on which everyone can agree – it is surely true to say that we do philosophy whenever we rationally reflect on the nature, purpose, meaning, justification or value of some general aspect of the world, rather than just a particular one. So, for example, we are not doing philosophy if we ask why someone built a temple where they did, or what Hamlet meant went he said, 'I am but mad north-north-west: when the wind is southerly I know a hawk from a handsaw.' But we are doing philosophy when we rationally dissect the purpose of religious worship, the meaning of metaphorical language or the nature of sanity. We can certainly use such reflection to illuminate specific cases, just as ethical reflection can help us think through a specific moral dilemma. But we would not be taking a philosophical approach to a moral problem if we confined ourselves only to the concrete case in front of us.

What that means is that, in practice, philosophy is unavoidable. You can't even reject philosophy without doing some first, because to reject it you have to think about its nature, value and purpose, which means doing it. Therefore, it could be argued that the statement 'philosophy is worthless' is a self-contradiction, as it is itself a philosophical position in need of a philosophical justification.

If we accept that there are at least some philosophical questions that inevitably arise, and it is worth spending some time trying to answer them, how can we set about doing so? Although different philosophers have adopted a number of different methods and strategies, arguably all of them can be divided into two camps, which reflect not just two approaches, but two basic philosophical temperaments. Right at the dawn of western philosophy, its two leading lights provided the templates for the two kinds of philosophy that were to follow. Those philosophers were Plato and Aristotle.

▶ The Platonic dream

Plato and Aristotle were contemporaries in Athens during the city's heyday. Plato was the older of the two and Aristotle was, for a time, his pupil at the Academy, a kind of cross between a university and private members' club set up by Plato around 387 BCE. Aristotle was a member for around 20 years before he went off and set up his own version, the Lyceum, around 335 BCE. Despite these biographical similarities, intellectually the two took very different approaches to their subjects.

Plato's outlook is memorably distilled in his allegory of the cave, in which the common mass of humanity is compared to prisoners in a cave, mistaking shadows on the wall for reality. The philosopher who leaves the cave and literally sees the light – the sun, representing ultimate reality – is at first blinded by it and on return to the cave cannot convince the others that he has discovered the truth while they live with illusions.

However, there is another analogy in the *Republic* of a divided line which, while lacking the vivid drama of the cave, in many ways more accurately reflects the spirit of Plato's philosophy. The line is divided into four parts, and each section represents a stage of human understanding, from the most primitive to the most advanced. The line can therefore be seen as a kind of ladder: the higher up you climb, the closer to true knowledge you get.

The bottom two rungs of the ladder both represent mere opinion (*doxa*). On the very lowest of these rungs, all we

Knowledge (*Epistēmē*)		Opinion (*Doxa*)	
True intelligence (*noēsis*)	Mathematical reasoning (*diaonoia*)	Belief (*pistis*)	Illusion (*eikasia*)
World of forms		Physical world	

▲ Plato's Divided Line

believe is illusion (*eikasia*). It is based on assumptions, all is second hand, and it isn't even based on the physical world as such but representations of it. The contemporary manifestation of *eikasia* is basing all your opinions on what you read and see in the media and online, without questioning its basis and without having any first-hand experience of the people and events described.

All Greek to me

The use of original Greek words when discussing ancient philosophy is not just a bit of intellectual showing-off. Translations are almost always not precise and when the word in question has a specific technical usage, sometimes more-or-less right isn't good enough. For example, although some think that 'happiness' is a harmless translation of *eudaimonia*, many scholars would say it is highly misleading, as it has little to do with positive mood. So it can be better to think of what a concept actually means in its original form and not in terms of what its best translation is.

One step up is belief (*pistis*). This is opinion that is first, not second hand, which would include beliefs formed by scientific or historical investigation. Why, then, does this still belong in the realm of mere opinion rather than genuine knowledge? For Plato, it is because such belief still rests on assumptions and, for him, the physical world is not the ultimate reality. The physical world is an imperfect thing where everything is always changing. In contrast, Plato believed that there also existed some kind of realm in which things were eternal and unchanging. This was the world of the forms. Forms are kinds of eternal, immutable ideals of which physical objects are merely individual, impermanent copies. So, for instance, there are millions of dogs, but only one form of the dog.

Whether or not Plato thought forms literally existed in some kind of world of their own, he clearly did believe that abstract concepts had a fixedness and permanence that physical objects lacked, so true knowledge had to concern itself with these, not the messy, changing world. So on the top two rungs of his ladder we find knowledge (*epistēmē*), which requires that we have first-hand knowledge of the forms. The second highest of these deals with mathematical reasoning (*diaonoia*). Numbers are forms that we can access, so through mathematics, we can get as high up the ladder as we can. But, still, we cannot reach the top rung because even mathematics has to make assumptions. Plato imagines that on the very top rung, where we achieve true intelligence (*noēsis*), we have first-hand knowledge of the real world of forms, which is based on no assumptions whatsoever. The only problem is, no one has got there yet. The divided line provides a map of the mountain, and Plato is confident that the peak exists, but no intellectual explorer has yet managed to find and ascend it.

Whether or not Plato's vision of true knowledge is sound, it set down the template for a style of philosophy that was to recur over the history of the subject to the present day. Plato's approach seeks to establish secure first principles, and to build a true picture of reality from these, through sound reasoning. This approach is often called foundationalist, for self-explanatory reasons. For Plato, these foundational first principles are not facts about the physical world, but immutable logical truths, ones that are established by reason alone, not experiment nor observation. They are universal and abstract. This manner of reasoning is called *a priori* – literally 'from what is prior'; in this case from what is prior to any facts about the world. It is not incidental that, for Plato, the closest thing we have got to this kind of philosophy is mathematics, for this is what provides the model for how philosophy should be: moving in clear, logical steps, providing proofs from principles which are timeless and whose truth does not depend on facts about the material world. It is not, however, the only approach, as Plato's own pupil was to show.

▶ The Aristotelian turn

To say Aristotle was a philosopher is, in modern language, to vastly understate the range of his thinking. He wrote on everything: biology, political science, metaphysics, rhetoric, art theory and so on. Unfortunately, little of his finished work has survived. What we now refer to as his books are in general collections of lecture notes. They are nonetheless remarkable for their subtlety of thought. If you read perhaps the most famous, the *Nichomachean Ethics*, one thing may strike you straight away: most of the sections begin with a survey of the prevalent views on a given subject. This might appear to be no more than a stylistic tic, but it points to a distinctive and important feature of Aristotle's thinking. He does not seek to establish secure, universal abstract *a priori* principles and reason from them. Rather, he starts by looking at the world as it is, at what people believe they know, and then works from there. This is *a posteriori* (literally 'from what comes after') or empirical reasoning, based on experience and the evidence from the real world, rather than on principles of logic and mathematics.

A posteriori reasoning does not promise the kind of precision and certainty of the *a priori*, but that is only because it does not believe that such precision and clarity is possible in most matters. The problem with *a priori* philosophy is the price it pays for basing itself on universal, abstract principles: it is not based on the messy reality of the real world. Therefore, it ends up telling us more about the logical relationship between concepts than it does about how things really are. So, for instance, in mathematics we have the clarity and certainty to say that $2 + 2 = 4$. But this tells you nothing about what happens when two things are put together with two other things in the real world. They might destroy, merge with or multiply each other. No principle of pure logic can tell you which of these outcomes is most likely.

Two traditions

Plato's style of reasoning has recurred throughout the history of philosophy, most notably in the seventeenth-century rationalism of Descartes, Leibniz and Spinoza, but also in the twentieth-century logicism of Bertrand Russell, which sought to base logic on secure mathematical foundations. Aristotle's approach has also echoed down the centuries, most notably in the eighteenth-century British empiricism of John Locke, Bishop Berkeley and David Hume, as well as the nineteenth-century American pragmatism of John Dewey, Charles Sanders Peirce and William James.

The two temperaments can therefore be fairly clearly distinguished. One leans more heavily on *a priori* arguments, the other on *a posteriori* ones. One focuses on universal, abstract principles, the other on particular, concrete ones. One looks to secure immutable foundations for knowledge, the other accepts that such a basis is almost certainly unattainable. One tends to see any imprecision as failing whereas the other embraces vagueness to the extent that it is appropriate to the subject.

But although there are clear and fundamental distinctions between these two temperaments, there is always a danger in philosophy that by putting thinkers into different categories, we overstate what these differences are. None of the greatest thinkers conform entirely to the stereotypes suggested by labels such as 'rationalist' and 'empiricist'. For instance, Plato may have aspired to the purity and certainty that knowledge of the forms would provide, but in his dialogues Socrates never attains such heights. As a result, he is constantly reminding us of the limits of our knowledge and encouraging us to live with belief that is less than certain. Socrates is portrayed as the wisest man in Athens precisely because the only thing he knows for certain is that he knows nothing else for certain.

Nor is it true that Aristotle rejected *a priori* methods altogether. Indeed, one of his most important contributions was to the development of logic, which is very much based on abstract principles, and which is devoid of any factual, empirical content. Rather, Aristotle simply maintained that 'it is a mark of the trained mind never to expect more precision in the treatment of any subject than the nature of that subject permits'. Plato would surely agree – who could not? The difference between Plato and Aristotle, and the thinkers who followed, is in the relative importance of *a priori* and *a posteriori* reasoning. The Platonic rationalist tends more to seek mathematical certainty and exactitude, whereas the Aristotelian empiricist expects more ambiguity, uncertainty and grey areas. That doesn't mean that the empiricist is vague about mathematics nor that the rationalist always insists that every distinction is clear and that all general principles are certain or useless.

◗ Truth and knowledge

Although most textbooks will happily run through the various theories concerning truth and knowledge that have dominated over the history of philosophy, I think that these general approaches or temperaments are more fundamental than particular theories. Take knowledge: it should be quite clear that you are going to have different families of theory depending on whether you take a broadly Platonic or Aristotelian approach. The Platonic urge is to sharply distinguish knowledge from belief, on the basis that to know something it is not enough that it is true – we must have some *guarantee* that it is true. Belief, in contrast, lacks proof or sufficient justification. This urge also manifests itself in how we define knowledge. The Platonic drive would be for a clear definition that enabled us to distinguish with precision between knowledge and opinion or belief.

From an Aristotelian perspective, however, things look rather different. The difference between knowledge and belief is likely to be a matter of degree, not absolute. The more grounds we have for our beliefs, the more justifiable it is to refer to them as containing knowledge. But nothing can ever be certain enough for us to claim 100% knowledge, and that is partly because there is no foundation strong enough to support all our beliefs. Rather than digging futilely for such foundations, therefore, the Aristotelian focuses instead on how well beliefs fit together, with both each other and the world. This approach can be described as holistic. It seeks coherence in our beliefs more than it does a single firm foundation. This approach extends to our definition of knowledge itself, which may not be precise. (In the next chapter we'll see how some take this further and claim that it is pointless even trying to come up with a clear definition.)

A similar split is manifest in approaches to truth. The Platonic temperament wants to establish 'the truth' as clear, certain and knowable. In particular, it seeks truths that are independent of time and place; truths of logic and mathematics that remain true for eternity. The Aristotelian alternative is that some things are more true than others, but very few things, or anything, have the status of eternal, unchanging truth. The best candidates we have for such things, such as the truths of mathematics, have this permanence only at the price of having nothing directly to say about the world we live in.

These issues are particularly important today because ours is a time of deep scepticism about both truth and knowledge. It is commonplace to hear people say that 'what's true for us may not be true for them', where 'them' could be people from another time, place or religious or political group. While people may accept that experts have some knowledge, there is a tendency to say that we hold different opinions, and that on most things that count we are all equally entitled to hold whatever these might be.

I think that the way to defeat the scepticism of the age – and the kind of postmodern thinking that follows – is not to try to defend notions of absolute truth and complete knowledge, but to explain how things are more complicated than that. Certainty is always a matter of degree and is never absolute.

Truth matters

If you're tempted by the idea that there is no objective truth, only different opinions, ask yourself if there is such a thing as 'the truth' about something really important, such as the Vietnam War. Not if you mean a single account that captures all that is true about it and leaves out nothing. But some accounts are fuller, more accurate and more truthful than others. And that is surely, obviously, *true*. If it were not, then we would have no good reason to doubt any official accounts from both sides, no good reason to look for evidence rather than just to opine from the bar stool and no good reason to value investigative reporting over internet gossip.

But from a philosophical point of view, there is always a technical gap between absolute certainty and the high degree of probability we are entitled to claim. It is this gap that the sceptic exploits. As A J Ayer wrote, the sceptic does not accept this and continues to insist on a Platonic standard for truth and knowledge. As a result, her 'demand for justification is such that it is necessarily true that it cannot be met'. If you accept the Platonic conception of truth, this is game, set and match, because it follows that there is no such thing as absolute truth or complete certainty. But for an Aristotelian, as for Ayer, this is a 'bloodless' victory because it only defeats conceptions of truth and knowledge that we should never have held in the first place.

Truth and knowledge have suffered the same fate as other mortal things that have been falsely elevated into God. Portray any human as a flawless saint and it is only a matter of time before we end up becoming disillusioned with the imperfect reality. Likewise, if we think of truth and knowledge as timeless, eternal absolutes, we are bound, eventually, to conclude that they are illusory or unattainable. If, however, we see them in less ideal terms, we will in the long run be better able to appreciate their importance and value. Not every philosopher would agree, of course, but that's why, to lay my cards on the table, I'm with Aristotle, not Plato.

3

Representing Reality

ALL THAT
MATTERS

Coming to a view about what truth and knowledge fundamentally involve can still leave you unable to say anything about what is actually true about our world. You may have a clear view of *what* knowledge is, but not yet understand *how* we can acquire it or what we really do know. We may understand that mathematical truths are abstract, theoretical, and so we can know them by the use of *a priori* reason alone. However, when it comes to more worldly matters such as how plants photosynthesize, armchair reflection won't get you very far. You need empirical observation and experiment. And when it comes to questions about what enables human life to flourish, things get even more complicated, because there is a strong evaluative component which is not *a priori* but seems to take us beyond mere observation, as we shall see in Chapter 10.

Setting aside *a priori* knowledge and evaluative claims for now, we are left with a large class of beliefs about what is often simply called 'the external world'. This comprises everything that we can perceive, either directly or indirectly through scientific measurement or experiment. What many philosophers have noticed over the centuries is that this external world does not come to us directly and unmediated. What we perceive is the world as it appears to our senses. But to what extent does this match the world as it is in itself? Furthermore, the claims we make about this world are made through language. But do our words map the world accurately? If so, how so?

Questions of language and perception are linked because they are both ways in which reality is represented to the human mind. Unless we have good reasons to think that these representations are accurate, it seems we have no grounds for believing that we have any reliable knowledge of the external world. So can we represent reality accurately?

▶ Perceiving the world

We don't need philosophers to tell us that 'things are not always what they seem', that 'appearances can be deceptive' and that 'you should not judge a book by its

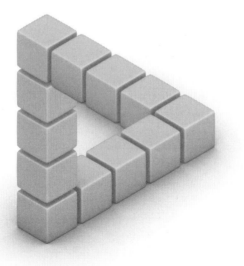

▲ The Penrose Triangle is named after its creator, mathematician Roger Penrose, who described it as 'impossibility in its purest form'.

cover'. We're all familiar with perceptual illusions, both human-made and natural, such as mirages, sweet foods tasting bitter if we are ill, echoes making distant voices sound close, and so on.

Common sense generally takes such deceptive perceptions to be the exception, not the rule. But philosophy goes further: is it not possible that we are deceived by our senses more often than not, perhaps even always? Remember Plato's allegory of the cave. If it is possible to imagine someone spending their whole life mistaking shadows for real objects, how do we know we're not in just that position?

This sceptical line of thought gets going once we realize that there are certain features of our sense perception which are at least as much reflections of our minds as they are of the world. Colour, sound, taste and smell come into this category. The redness of a tomato is the result of how our eyes and brains react to certain wavelengths of light, and it is quite within the bounds of possibility that another species could experience red as we do blue and vice versa. We also know that only some parts of the light spectrum are visible to us, so it is also possible that other creatures could see infrared, or not see blue at all. The same is true of some other senses. Dogs can hear things we can't, and what sounds high pitched to us could be a deep bass to other animals.

Filtering reality

Some ways in which the world appears different to different people are common and obvious, such as the fact that we don't all taste and smell things in the same way, with some of us finding too bitter, sweet, spicy or sour what others find mild. Others are more exotic. For instance, some people have a strange condition called synaesthesia, in which the usual sense perceptions are jumbled up. They may see music as a pattern of colours, or hear colours as musical notes.

At first sight, this need not be too troubling. In John Locke's taxonomy, these sense-dependent features of the world can be lumped together as the *secondary properties* of objects. They are not properties that the object inherently has; rather, they are properties that objects give rise to only when they encounter the human, or similar, sense perception system. Nonetheless, we can also say that objects have some *primary qualities*, ones that do not depend on how we perceive them but which are really there. So, for example, a basketball may look red or brown, depending on who or what is looking at it. But whether it will fit through a hoop depends solely on it and the hoop, not on anything about the human mind.

So it looks like there is a clear difference between mind-dependent and mind-independent reality, which we can know. This position is known as *realism*. But as Locke's contemporary Bishop Berkeley pointed out, in what way are primary qualities mind-independent? When we talk of the size, shape and solidity of objects, what are we talking about other than the way they appear? Strip away all that comes to us through the senses and you are left not with 'matter', as Locke thought, but just 'something, we know not what'.

Berkeley's solution to this problem was to collapse primary and secondary qualities into a single category. Both are varieties of *idea*, and both exist only as perceptions. This is the radical thesis called *idealism*: there is no mind-independent reality at all. To say that something exists is to say that at least one mind could, in principle at least, perceive it. '*Esse est percipi*' – to be is to be perceived. The common-sense idea that there is a difference between appearance and reality has become the counterintuitive claim that appearance *is* reality.

Realism and idealism are the two major families of positions, and both contain members of almost infinite variety. One of the most distinguished is Kant's transcendental idealism. Unlike Berkeley, Kant did think there was a 'noumenal' world of things-inthemselves-independent of our minds. However, he also thought that we could not possibly have any access to it. Our knowledge, therefore, has to be confined to the 'phenomenal' world of appearances. What's more, how this phenomenal world appears turns out to say more about how our minds work than the way the world is. Time and space, for instance, are the ways in which we frame the world: they are not properties of the world itself.

The debate over the extent to which the world we perceive is the world as it is or merely as it seems to us has not come to an end, and it appears in many forms. But there is also another great historical debate about how we represent the world: through our use of language.

▶ Picture this

In folk philosophy, language works in a reasonably straightforward way: words essentially *refer* to things in the world. That is to say, there are things in the world and words label them. But perhaps this is too simple. How, for instance, do children in the English-speaking West learn that 'lion' refers to a real animal rather than to the pictures of the animal they learn the word from? The child somehow manages to make the correct assumption about what the word labels, even though it is by no means unambiguous.

The problem applies to any view that says the meaning of words is given by some kind of mental picture, which is what Wittgenstein thought in his early philosophy. But in time he realized that no picture can ever capture the meaning of a word. For example, you know what 'dog' means and could use the word perfectly well if you came across an unfamiliar breed. But you can't possibly be matching real dogs to your mental image of dog, not least because there are more breeds than you can picture and they all look different anyway.

The picture theory struggles even more when you think of all the words that aren't concrete nouns. What picture, still or moving, for example, would capture the meaning of 'run'? A person running, you might think. But what tells you the meaning isn't 'hurrying' or 'racing' instead? And what in the picture enables you to apply the word to greyhounds when its motions are completely different? Start thinking about abstract nouns – such as intelligence, anger, complexity – as well as adjectives, adverbs and propositions, and the idea that an image can capture their meaning looks less and less plausible.

Could the problem be that we have left out half of what makes a word a word? The picture theory focuses on *reference*: what in the world words refer to. But words also have a *sense*, a definition. Gottlob Frege made this distinction clear with his most famous example of 'the morning star' and 'the evening star'. These have different senses. One refers to a bright celestial body visible in the evenings, the other a bright celestial body visible in the mornings. But both refer to the same planet: Venus. Similarly, the meanings of 'first president of the USA' and 'George Washington' differ, but they refer to the same person.

In some respects, it is clearly true that words have both sense and reference. But we do not understand words by knowing all they refer to, nor do we acquire mastery of language by learning a list of words' senses, in the form of definitions. There are many words we use quite happily and correctly, but which we would struggle to define. The way language actually functions seems not to depend on us having a clear understanding of either sense or reference. So what else are we missing?

▶ Language games

Probably the most influential theory of language of the last hundred years came from Wittgenstein in his later philosophy, after he rejected the picture theory set out in his *Tractatus Logico-Philosophicus*. His revised view was not just a new way to think about language: it was a new way to think about philosophy.

Wittgenstein believed that 'philosophical problems arise when language goes on holiday'. But if philosophy is a victim of linguistic vacationing, it is also the means of its remedy, for 'Philosophy is a struggle against the bewitchment of our understanding by the resources of our language'. How, then, does language 'bewitch' or 'go on holiday'? The general thought is that certain grammatical features of language mislead us about how things really are. The most obvious examples are nouns. With a few exceptions, every complete English sentence must contain a noun (or pronoun). But what is a noun? The standard answer is that it is *a thing* of some kind. That is the root of the problem. 'A thing' implies a singular object. But if you think about all sorts of nouns, it is not at all obvious that they refer to singular objects at all. Just consider this list: love, knowledge, stress, weather, ignorance, pride, prejudice, information, *joie de vivre*.

Category mistakes

Gilbert Ryle imagined a tourist asking a taxi driver to show him the University of Oxford. After being driven past the Bodleian Library, All Souls College, the Ashmolean Museum and so on, the tourist asks, 'Yes, but where is the university?' His mistake is to think that the university is a singular object when in reality it is an institution made up of its members, its colleges, its buildings and so on. We make a category mistake whenever we confuse one type of thing (such as a collection) with another (such as an object).

Apply the lesson of Wittgenstein to the question of truth and knowledge that we looked at in the previous chapter and you can see what the problem might be. Philosophers go looking for the nature of 'truth' and 'knowledge' as though these words refer to something singular and definable. But just because we have a single word it does not mean that there is a single thing – real or abstract – that it labels. In fact, Wittgenstein argued in his late work that language never works like this. You know what a word means when you know how to use it, not what its definition is. That is why we can understand and use all sorts of words that we struggle to define clearly if we are put on the spot and asked to do so.

A line of thought like this led to the creation of the 'ordinary language' strand of philosophy in Oxford after the Second World War. In effect, it asserted that the meanings of concepts such as 'truth' and 'knowledge' were to be found not in philosophy but by looking at how the words were used in normal, everyday speech. In a curious reversal of the traditional relationship between philosophy and the general public, the philosopher's job was now to look to the masses for enlightenment, not vice versa.

The idea that we have to already know what words mean before we can give a philosophical account of them goes back to Agrippa in the first century after Christ, but was given its contemporary formulation by Roderick Chisholm in 1973, who called it the 'problem of the criterion'. For example, we want to define 'knowledge', so we come up with some kind of definition, such as the idea that knowledge is justified true belief. But we cannot know whether this definition is correct unless we already know the difference between genuine cases of knowledge and mere belief, so we can see if the definition applies correctly. So we have to know what knowledge is before we can say whether we have correctly defined what it means.

Definitions may still be worth seeking, in that they might help crystallize and clarify the fuzziness of normal, tacit understanding. On the other hand, as Wittgenstein seemed to suggest, definitions might distort, because they seek to attach clear and precise conditions to the use of words when, in reality, the meaning of words is always to be found in their use, and this use cannot be reduced to a set of simple rules.

▶ Carving nature at the joints

Whatever theory of language you end up agreeing with (if any), there is a common worry that the mere fact that we cannot describe the world in anything other than words means we are inevitably unable to describe the world as it is. Language is a human construction, not a natural phenomenon. But that does not mean language is no guide at all to reality. The world is not a kind of undifferentiated dough, with language as a cookie cutter able to create any shapes in it. A much better analogy is the one Plato offered in the *Phaedrus,* of a butcher. For language to be useful, it must follow the principle 'of division into species according to the natural formation, where the joint is, not breaking any part as a bad carver might.' If language didn't carve nature at the joints, we wouldn't be able to use it effectively.

Carving up the world

Different languages carve up the world in different ways. Whereas English has the single verb 'to be', Spanish has *ser* and *estar*, distinguishing between (roughly speaking) the inherent and relational properties of a thing. In English *we know*, whereas in French *nous connaissons* or *nous savons*, depending on whether we are acquainted with something or we have understanding of it. So, when we use language to describe the world, we are reflecting how we carve it up as well as how it actually is.

Once again, it seems that philosophy falls short if we expect certainty and precision from it, but it can serve us well if we have more modest expectations. Our perceptions of the world do not enable us entirely to penetrate through appearances into the world as it is in itself, nor does any human language represent the world with complete accuracy. But both our language and our senses could not enable us to manipulate and get around this complicated world unless there were a decent degree of fit between world, words and perceptions. How sceptical we should be depends in part on a judgement of how loose this fit can afford to be. And the answer to that may again go back to temperament. Just as some people are only comfortable in well-tailored clothes whereas others prefer baggier attire, how much slack we're prepared to give philosophy may well depend on personality. The irony of this, of course, is that people who think that our human nature and understanding shapes the way we understand and perceive the world too much do so not because of the way the world is, but because of the way they are.

4

Ultimate Reality

ALL THAT
MATTERS

Once you get down to the most basic of philosophical questions, it can seem like a long climb back up to the kinds of questions that led us to them in the first place. But now our journey is beginning to take us back to more worldly questions. Having considered what truth and knowledge are, and then how we get to them, we can now ask what we actually know about our universe.

You might think this is not a philosophical question, but a scientific one, and there are some eminent scientists who would agree. 'Philosophy is dead,' declared Stephen Hawking in 2011. 'Philosophers have not kept up with modern developments in science.' The biologist Lewis Wolpert is even more forthright: 'If philosophy hadn't existed,' he once said to me, making a small exception for Aristotle, 'what would we not know? The answer is that it wouldn't have made the slightest difference.'

We will come to the question of whether or not philosophy has contributed to our understanding of the nature of science and its methods in the next chapter. But, first, we need to ask whether it has aided our understanding of the fundamental nature of reality, through its study of metaphysics. As its name suggests, metaphysics sits one level up from physics. Physicists try to understand the laws that govern the workings of the universe. Metaphysicians try to understand the basic principles and mechanisms that these laws need to assume.

For example, physicists deal with the question of what matter fundamentally comprises, be it atoms, sub-atomic particles, strings or some kind of energy.

But even if this work were completed and we had the 'theory of everything' craved by scientists, philosophical questions would remain. And one of these we've already come across: is this stuff the universe is made of mind–independent or not? So although physicists might be able settle the dispute between string theory and loop quantum gravity, it takes metaphysicians to settle the dispute between idealism and realism. Both are, in some sense, questions about the most basic nature of reality, but only the scientific one is an empirical question to be settled by experiment.

When scientists like Wolpert and Hawking claim that philosophy is dead, they generally mean that metaphysics in particular is dead. The objection appears to be that science investigates the fundamental nature of reality with rigour and evidence, and that any other discipline that attempts to do the same without the painstaking research, experiment and mathematical calculation has got to be fraudulent; intellectual puzzles that tell us nothing about how the universe really works. But these objections miss the point that metaphysics is not doing the same thing as science at all, even though its basic subject matter – the fundamental nature of reality – appears to be the same. Whether string theory or loop quantum gravity is true is just not the same kind of question as whether reality is mind-independent or not.

Having said that, it is no bad thing for philosophers to consider the possibility that at least part of what they do is empty, useless and past its sell-by date. If we believe that metaphysics is not dead, we have to show what philosophy can contribute which science cannot. And perhaps there is one issue in particular where philosophy really does have something to add: causation.

▲ Does everything happen for a reason?

▶ What is a cause?

There is a truth about our universe so basic that we usually take it completely for granted: things happen because they have causes. If the phone rings, rain falls or you get ill, you just know there is some cause (or causes) that explains why, even if you don't know what this cause is. Things do not happen for no reason at all.

Escaping destiny

To say everything happens for a reason is not the same as saying that everything has a *purpose*. If a lump of cliff crumbles and crushes a person below, that does not mean this happened because of destiny or some divine plan. All it means is that there are physical explanations for why the cliff did not hold together and that if we understood completely the natural forces at work we would understand why the erosion led to such catastrophic consequences.

However, what look like common-sense assumptions about causation turn out to be horrendously complicated if you try to unpack what they mean. Take the issue of what it means to say that X caused Y. The contemporary philosopher Ted Honderich likes to use an apparently simple example of a fire. The obvious answer to the question of what caused this might be that a match was struck. But if you think about it, that is not enough to have caused the fire. It was also necessary that the match and box were dry, that oxygen was present, that combustible material was to hand and that someone intended the fire to start or was negligent enough to let one start by accident.

There is, thus, a difference between the *full causal story* – a comprehensive account of everything that needed to happen for the event Y to come about – and what we usually identify as 'the cause' or 'the causes'. In identifying some particular part of this account as 'the cause', say the lighting of the match, we are therefore simply attending to that part of the story that most concerns us. We are not identifying the 'true' cause.

This might sound nit-picky, evoking the sighed response familiar to philosophers when others do not share their precision (*'You know what I mean . . .'*). We all know that fire requires oxygen and so forth. We don't need to say that. What we need to identify as the cause is what made the difference between the dry, oxygen-filled room continuing as it was and burning down. And as we'll see when we come to the question of free will shortly, comprehending the full causal story can change the way we understand things.

Going back to the fire, perhaps the problem is that we haven't stated clearly what it means to say X caused Y. You could try 'Y happened as a result of X', but that really does little more than rephrase the original causal claim; it doesn't actually explain it. So we need something more specific, and therefore also artificial sounding. For example, you might say X caused Y if X was both necessary and sufficient for Y to occur. This also has the advantage that X can be a single event or a set of conditions. So, for example, the full cause of the fire has to include all the things that were together necessary for the fire to take place, but also sufficient, in that nothing else was needed.

This account is similar to one of the most popular ways of defining causation philosophically, by means of counterfactuals. A counterfactual is simply a claim about what would have happened under different conditions. So to say X caused Y is to say that Y would not have occurred if X had not occurred. This seems beautifully simple and true. The fire would not have started if the match had not been struck, and therefore the striking of the match is rightly identified as the cause.

However, both the counterfactual and necessary and sufficient condition views face similar problems. The first is the question of whether they are really informative definitions or still just ways of rephrasing, albeit perhaps helpful ones. Isn't 'Y would not have occurred if X had not occurred' simply another way of saying 'Y happened as a result of X'? What does this add?

A deeper problem is that neither seems to solve the problem that the full causal story ends up being just too big. The full set of necessary and sufficient conditions for the starting of the fire includes not just the presence of oxygen, dryness and so on, but the fact that the striker of the match did not miss her bus that morning, or that the shop that sold the matches held stock that day. Similarly, it may be true that had the match not been struck, the fire would not have started, but it is also true that had the parents of the person striking the match not met many decades ago, it wouldn't have started either.

So it turns out to be very difficult to come up with an informative definition of what it really means for one thing to cause another. But it gets worse. It seems even harder to justify our belief that things do really cause each other in the first place.

▶ Believing in a cause

Whatever account we give of causation, it would seem to involve some idea of *necessary connection*. To say that X caused Y is to say that, in some sense, Y *had to happen*, given that X did. Even if we struggle to define clearly what the nature of this necessary connection is, it seems obviously to be there, and our ability to move around in the world and function in it depends upon us spotting such connections. To take a quotidian example, if you want a jacket for walking and you have a choice between a blue cotton one and a red waterproof-lined one, you need to know that there is a necessary connection between the material it is made of and its ability to keep you dry, but that there is no such necessary connection with its colour.

The philosophical problem is that although we all know such necessary connections exist, and may seem obvious, it is remarkably difficult to explain how we spot them. You might think we simply *observe* that certain fabrics keep you dry whereas others don't, while we don't see any evidence that an item of clothing's colour affects its water resistance. But, in fact, as David Hume pointed out, we see no such thing. All we observe are regularities, one thing following another or accompanying another. But we do not observe any necessary connection between them.

Take a very simple example: you light a gas flame under a pot of water and it comes to the boil. Watch carefully. Where is this necessary connection you claim to be able to detect? Isn't it the case that all you have actually ever seen is a flame under a pan being followed by the water coming to the boil? You assume – rightly – that there is a necessary connection, but you certainly don't see what that connection is. If you did, you probably wouldn't need to study physics to work out why the water boils.

If you don't *see* the connection, don't you at least *infer* it? Perhaps. But this inference does not look very robust. It is basically of the form:

Whenever a hot enough heat source is placed under a pot of water, it comes to the boil.

Without such a heat source, the water does not come to the boil.

Therefore, there is a necessary connection between the placing of the heat source and the boiling of the water.

From a logical point of view, this is a very weak argument. First of all, it faces the same problem as any argument based on a generalization from observation, namely that nothing that has happened can logically prove that the same things will continue to happen. People believed all swans were white on the basis they had never seen one of any other colour, only later to discover black ones in the Antipodes. Arguments that generalize from past experience are known as inductive arguments, and all of them face this 'problem of induction'. As, arguably, all claims about how the world is, including all scientific claims, are based on inductive arguments, this is no small problem.

The uses of scepticism

Sceptical arguments can work in one of two ways. One is to undermine a belief, encouraging or forcing us to abandon it. Another is not to undermine the belief, but simply to point to the limits of its justification. This may lead us to rethink either the nature of what it is we believe in or the nature of justification itself. Coming to see that a belief is not quite as firmly established as we believed does not always mean we should just abandon it.

But what's worse for causation is that even if we solved the problem of induction, we would still not necessarily have justified belief in necessary connection. So, for instance, even if we could prove that 'all pans of water will come to the boil if a high enough heat source is applied to them', this would still not justify the claim that there is a *necessary* connection between the application of heat and boiling. The claim that something is *always* the case is not the same as the claim that it is *necessarily* the case. It is always the case that the sun rises in the morning, but it ain't necessarily so: one day the sun will die out and there will be no sunrise.

It's important to recognize that although Hume was sceptical about the grounds and justification of causal reasoning, he clearly did believe that causes are real and that all our reasoning about how the world works depends on us assuming they are real and being able to identify them. His kind of 'mitigated scepticism' need not, and perhaps cannot, lead us to give up belief in ideas that we entirely depend upon in order to live in and think about the world. And perhaps the best example of that comes with free will.

Free will

The idea that we have free will seems to be central to how we conceive of ourselves as thinking, conscious beings. What makes us different from robots or simpler animals is that not only do we act, we make real choices. Human beings are always choosing to turn their backs on social norms, doing new things and defying expectation.

Even the most intelligent dolphin, in contrast, is always found in a school, just doing what dolphins do.

But what does it mean to say we have free will? Once again, let's start with the common-sense understanding. To say you have free will means that you can select among a range of possible options, that your choice is not forced, and that, whatever you choose, it was in your power to have done otherwise, had you wished.

This sounds clear enough. But go back to the idea of causation. Are we saying here that having free will means that the cause of your action was your own decision? That might be fair enough, but does your decision describe the full causal story of your choice? To see if it does, we need to know more about how that decision arose.

At one extreme, we might want to suggest that the whole point about a free choice is that it has no cause other than itself. Free will is precisely the ability to make a decision free from any other influence. But a little reflection should show that this can't be right. If choices just came from nowhere they would be random, not free. If there is no reason why you chose coffee instead of tea, and this is a paradigm of free will, then to have free will is no more than the ability to flip a metaphorical coin in your head.

What's more, it seems obvious that meaningful choices do not just emerge from nowhere. They arise within internal and external constraints. Externally, they are responses to situations in which a certain range of possibilities has presented itself. In most cafés and bars, for instance, you can choose tea or coffee, but not absinthe. Internally, there are also preferences and desires that have grown over time, as the result of both nature and nurture. If I choose coffee, it is because I like it, and that reflects facts about me which are in part explained by both my biological nature and my biographical history.

If you start to fill out this causal story, however, something strange happens. Your free choice ends up looking, if not entirely inevitable, then simply another link in a chain. Given who and what you are, what has brought you to this point and the options you face, you are bound to make the choice you do.

This does not mean that you were somehow fated to do what you did from birth; that life is like a line of dominoes and once you push the first one over it is only a matter of time before each one falls in a predetermined sequence. This could be true, but it is unlikely to be so, simply because we now know that nature doesn't work like this. Chaotic and quantum effects mean that nature is not like a piece of clockwork. So it is not the case that any choice we make is one we were always bound to make because of our past histories. Choices become inevitable only at the point at which they are made: they were not always so.

Nor does it imply some kind of fate pulling us in the direction of a future outcome. This is the rather mystical or supernatural idea that we each of us have a destiny and that nature, or the gods, conspires to make sure that whatever we try to do, we will always be pulled back to our predetermined path.

So if inevitability is a matter of being neither pushed nor pulled to act in a certain way that was never going to be any different, what does it mean? It means that, given what has actually happened to date, whether or not that was always going to happen, we can only do what we end up doing at the time. Your choice in any given situation is simply the product of the options available, your temperament, the mood you're in, the beliefs you have and so on.

It's important to stress that this does not mean your choice is entirely predictable, even in theory. Any event whose causes are even a little complicated is unpredictable to some extent. Think about how poor predictions can be for the weather or the economy. Yet in comparison with the human mind, these are fairly simple systems operating within fairly well-understood laws.

At the same time, there is clearly a large degree of predictability to our choices. Indeed, our ability to make plans, for ourselves and others, depends on us being reasonably predictable. Knowing what others would do or would like is what enables us to negotiate in business, make social arrangements, surprise people with presents and so on. We may find people dull if they are too predictable, but anyone whose preferences, desires and choices changed with the weather would be impossible to be with, or even to get to know.

If we go back to the common-sense definition of free will, this seems to fit in all but one very important respect. In such a situation, you are indeed selecting among a range of possible options and your choice is not forced on you by anyone else. But it no longer seems true to say that it was in your power to have done otherwise, had you wished. The only way you could have acted differently was if your decision-making included some kind of capacity to avoid inevitability by generating random variations. But, as we've seen, this wouldn't be a kind of free will worth having.

If all this is true, then some people are worried. Doesn't it mean that we don't have free will after all? This takes us back to the idea of what sceptical arguments can do. They can be debunking, showing us that cherished beliefs are false. But they can also lead us to revise what we think our cherished beliefs really are. In the case of free will, this is how compatibilists argue. They say that it is true that all our choices are, in the sense described, inevitable consequences of prior causes. But, they insist, this is compatible with us having the kind of free will that matters. To put it negatively, why would anyone value the capacity to make decisions out of the blue, ones that are not caused by who and what we are? It is good, not bad, that our choices flow from the individuals we are, and not from some random power of generation.

On this view, to be free is not to be free from the normal chain of causation that governs everything in the universe. It is to be free from the tyranny of others, of the malign influence of brain-washers, or the distorting power of certain drugs. In some sense, perhaps, we are robots, biological machines operating entirely within the laws of nature. But as long as we are autonomous machines, left literally to our own devices, we are free. For what else could freedom mean but this?

▶ Back to reality

Free will is a good example of how issues of real life have connections with far more abstract questions of philosophy. Talk of the nature of causation, of striking matches and fires, may sound arcane and irrelevant to real life, but without a good understanding of what causes are, and what it means to say something is caused by something else, we can't think clearly about what it means to be free.

Of course, what I have said merely scratches the surface of involved and complex debates, to which there are no neat and easy answers. And this invites the question, 'what is it that enables science to come to firmer conclusions than philosophy?' We have talked about what knowledge and truth are, how we know, and even some of what we know. But surely the most successful means that humans have devised for getting knowledge of the world is not philosophy, but science. Why, and how, is that so?

Modelling the Universe

Metaphysics often seems speculative and inconclusive, but then so does much contemporary physics. Physicists debate whether we live in just one of an infinite number of multiverses; whether the universe will expand forever or eventually collapse; whether quantum theory shows that causation is truly probabilistic or whether it is deterministic but unknowable; whether quantum theory and general relativity can be reconciled by the postulate that matter is fundamentally composed of one-dimensional strings; and so on. The distinction between sober, hard science and extravagant, speculative philosophy appears to be at the very least blurred, if not entirely illusory.

Yet it is generally agreed that 'the scientific method' is an especially powerful means of generating knowledge of the world, and that scientific claims are fundamentally different from philosophical ones. This is because, even in cutting-edge physics, conclusions are reached by a combination of experiment, observation and empirical testing. This allows for a degree of convergence of opinion among scientists which, while not complete (especially in fundamental physics), is much greater than that achieved in philosophy. This may be a somewhat simplified picture, but to the extent that it is true, how is it that science can achieve the kind of success that philosophy can only envy?

▶ Induction

Just as there are often no eureka moments when scientific breakthroughs are made, so there no eureka moment when the scientific method was itself discovered. Nevertheless, if any single person has

▲ *An Experiment on a Bird in the Air Pump* by Joseph Wright 'of Derby', 1768.

a claim to being the originator of what we now think of as experimental science it is Francis Bacon. Bacon was both a scientist and a philosopher of science, and in his major work, *Novum Organum*, he set out the basic principles for how science has been done ever since.

Bacon put forward the now commonplace idea that science should proceed according to an experimental method starting from observation. Significantly, he argued that the method of inference to be used to move from observation to hypothesis has to be *inductive*, not *deductive*. To understand the difference, and why it is so important, think about why you would believe that I have a heart – literally, that is. In reality, you wouldn't have to think about why you believe this. But if you were to formalize your reasoning you might come to say something like: we know all humans have hearts, and you're a human, so you must have one. That sentence is in fact a pretty well-formed deductive argument, the structure of which becomes clearer if we break it up into three lines:

All humans have hearts.

You are a human.

Therefore, you have a heart.

In this argument, the first two lines are *premises*, that is to say, the facts or statements that form the basis of the inference. From these two premises, a conclusion is generated, which is the last line. What makes this argument a good *deductive* one is that the conclusion *necessarily* follows from the premises. That is to say, if the premises are true, the conclusion *must* be true. Just as two plus two must equal four, so the conjunction of the two premises must lead to the conclusion: if all humans have hearts and you are a human, you *must* have a heart.

That means, of course, that the conclusion is only as secure or certain as the premises. It *must* be true only *if* the premises are true. And that turns out to be the reason why science cannot be fundamentally based on deduction. Take a look at that argument again. It contains the claim 'all humans have hearts'. But how do we know this? We haven't X-rayed or done postmortems on all humans. So it seems the most we can claim is that all humans examined so far have hearts. But then, if we make that our first premise, the deduction no longer works:

All humans examined so far have hearts.

You are a human.

Therefore . . .

Therefore nothing. Unless we have examined you to see if you have a heart, it does not follow *by necessity* from our observation of others that you have a heart too. And let's not forget that it is becoming increasingly possible for a human not to have a heart: some people may soon have mechanical heart substitutes instead.

Now you might think this is again a matter of being picky, because surely it is overwhelmingly probable, to the point of being almost certain, that you do indeed have a heart. So can't we reason:

All humans examined so far have hearts.

You are a human.

Therefore, it is almost certain you have a heart too.

In one sense, this is perfectly good argument. But it is not a good *deductive* one, because the uniformity of past observations does not make any conclusion about even the probability of other observations *necessarily* true. We have already come across the example of the time when, in Britain, all swans observed thus far had been white. But that did not make it almost certain that all swans were white, as the discovery of black ones in the Antipodes showed.

What Bacon realized was that science could never progress on the basis of deductive reasoning because it ultimately generalizes from a limited number of observations in a way that is not deductively valid. That does not mean that science is irrational or illogical. It simply means that the scientist should formulate general principles on the basis of particular findings, and that as the confidence we have in the truth of these general principles increases, the more particular experiments are found to be in accordance with them. That means scientific claims are never completely certain and they are always open to refutation if an observation is made that contradicts them.

Mathematics vs. science

Mathematics achieves certainty at the cost of making claims not about the real world, only about numbers. Physical science has the great advantage of being able to say things about how the real world works, but to gain this advantage it has to give up any claim to certainty. A perpetual state of provisonality is the price science pays for being able to make progress. So you could say that the strength of physical science is tied up with its weakness.

▶ Wanting to be wrong

Ever since Bacon, philosophers of science have, in various ways, tried to be more precise about just how this inductive method works. One of the most famous was Karl Popper, who argued that what makes a claim scientific is that it is *falsifiable*. That is to say, every scientific claim implies a hypothetical discovery which, if made, would show that it is wrong. So, for instance, if it is claimed that the speed of sound is 343.2 metres per second, that implies that an experiment which proved that sound actually travelled at a different speed would prove it wrong.

This feature of falsifiability is what makes science evidence based. In contrast, take a theological claim, for instance that the wafer in the Catholic communion ceremony is changed into the body of Christ. This is not a claim that if you tested the wafer, you would find it contained human body cells with the DNA of Jesus. That means that you cannot falsify the Catholic doctrine of transubstantiation by experiment. It becomes a matter of faith, which is protected from the scrutiny of reason and experience.

It is the great strength of science that it only makes claims that can be tested and shown to be false. Nothing is sacred in science except the fact that nothing is sacred. Popper took this further and claimed that the whole process of doing science is based on trying to prove things false, not correct. Science works, he argued, by a process of conjecture and refutation. First, a scientist comes up with a conjecture, a hypothesis, that she believes explains a natural phenomenon. The next stage is to conduct experiments to see if that conjecture can be proved wrong. Every time an experiment fails to prove the conjecture wrong, the confidence we have that it is correct increases. This simply puts Bacon's inductive principle in negative terms. Bacon believed that as more particular experiments are found to be in accordance with general principles, the confidence we have in the truth of them increases. Popper's idea is that as more particular experiments fail to be in discordance with general principles, the confidence we have in the truth of them increases.

Many scientists have argued that Popper completely misdescribes the way they actually work. But even if they think scientists do not spend most of their time actively seeking to falsify their theories, most agree that the fact that theories are falsifiable is crucial.

▶ Method under fire

From the middle to the late part of the twentieth century in particular, philosophers and sociologists of science have increasingly come to question the extent to which science really is a pure, rational, evidence-based form of enquiry. What they have in common is a tendency to see science as something undertaken in particular social contexts, reflecting the agendas and biases of the time. They also are keen to show how scientists are not dispassionate, motiveless automata, but real human beings with biases, weaknesses and blind spots. At their extreme, such thinkers propagate the frankly implausible view that science is a 'mere' construct, and that the claims of scientists are no more 'valid' or 'true' than the claims of shamans or priests. But at their more sober, they have had interesting things to say about how science works.

Take the most popular book in the history of the philosophy of science, Thomas Kuhn's *The Structure of Scientific Revolutions*. Kuhn challenged two central orthodoxies of thinking about science. The first is that progress in science is essentially linear and cumulative. Science is building up a picture of nature and every new discovery is like another piece in the jigsaw. The second is that all that scientists are doing is basically looking at the puzzle which is the natural world and trying to see what pieces fit where.

Kuhn argued that, for most of the time, scientific research follows a programme within a general framework that seems to work. There is a 'paradigm': a more or less clear and widely shared set of assumptions about what the problems are and how to solve them. The time during which the paradigm is accepted and leads to fruitful research is a phase Kuhn called 'normal science'. However, what inevitably happens eventually is that results emerge that do not fit the paradigm. Contrary to what Popper argued, scientists do not immediately reject the paradigm as falsified. Rather, they struggle to make the anomalies compatible with the established theories. But these attempts at holding things together cannot be sustained indefinitely. Normal science reaches a crisis, and the paradigm has to be rejected. The search then starts for a new paradigm, and once it is found, a new phase of normal science can begin. To go back to the jigsaw metaphor, it is as though each period of normal science sees scientists working on the same puzzle, but, eventually, too many pieces are missing or cannot be fitted together, and so the puzzle has to be thrown away and a new one selected to be worked on instead.

The strongest objection to Kuhn's theory is history: this just does not seem to accurately describe how science has actually progressed. General relativity, for instance, may have required a deep rethinking of classical physics, and quantum theory in turn led to a revision of how general relativity was understood. But even in these cases there was not a complete overturning of the old order. If the popular mythology of science overstates its continuities, Kuhn seemed to exaggerate the discontinuities.

Others who have taken up these ideas have been even more extreme. Paul Feyerabend, for instance, argued in *Against Method* that there was no such thing as the scientific method at all. The way real scientists conduct their research is anarchic and resists any attempt to reduce it to a procedure with clear steps and progressions. Again, although there is surely some hyperbole here, it is important to realize that science has elements of art and craft, and that many researchers freely admit that they follow hunches, trust some results more than others and don't always know why they are drawn to research some directions rather than others. This may not be anarchy, but nor is it the ordered process of conjecture and refutation proposed by Popper.

The philosophy of science may have failed to identify clearly what the scientific method is and what makes scientific knowledge distinctive and valuable. But to go back to the guiding lesson of Aristotle, this should not necessarily be seen as damning failure. We do understand science better if we come to recognize that science is inductive and evidence based, but defies reduction to a straightforward method; that the objectivity of science is compromised but not necessarily defeated by social and psychological factors. To understand better is valuable even when we cannot understand perfectly: a principle that applies to both scientific knowledge and our knowledge of science.

Surveying the Heavens

In London's Carlton House Terrace, not far from Buckingham Palace and the Houses of Parliament, sits the headquarters of the Royal Society, founded in 1660 as one of the world's first scientific academies. It is also the publisher of one of the world's oldest scientific journals, the name of which reflects an important fact about the development of human knowledge: *Philosophical Transactions*.

Natural science is the child of philosophy, so much so that it has often borne the name of the parent. 'Natural philosophy' persisted as the name for what we now call science from the fifteenth until the nineteenth century. That science has grown into the strong, autonomous discipline it is today is perhaps due to an extremely long period of gestation, followed by a lengthy infancy.

Experimental philosophy

As an example of how recent the division between science and philosophy is, consider that in the 1640s a group of thinkers including Robert Hooke, Robert Boyle, John Locke, John Wilkins and Christopher Wren met as the Oxford Experimental Philosophy Club to discuss what we would now recognize as science. Today, one of the most popular recent movements in philosophy has advocated incorporating more empirical data and testing of claims. Its name? Experimental philosophy.

Science's core strength was certainly present in its parent's DNA, a nature which nurture reinforced. That strength is a way of thinking that we now take for granted but which was at the time revolutionary. We can call this *the naturalistic turn*, and it marks the birth of philosophy. Western philosophy began in Ancient Greece when people first started to try to think about how the world worked by a combination of reason and observation, not myth or pure speculation. They looked no further than the world to understand the world, believing that nature itself could contain the answers to our questions about how it worked.

Early efforts were not very successful. For instance, today we find the biology of Aristotle often comically poor, even though his work in other areas is still compelling. It took nearly 2,000 years before the likes of Bacon really worked out how to do experimental science, which finally emerged blinking from the philosophical womb.

Why did it take so long? One reason is perhaps because it took time for divine, supernatural causes and purposes to be fully excised from human understanding of the natural world. It was only when 'natural philosophy' became fully 'naturalized' that it could become 'natural science'. Only when 'natural science' became simply 'science' could its natural nature finally be taken for granted.

But if this is even roughly correct, two related questions arise. The first is why religious ways of thinking still persist. If religion were nothing more than an unwelcome residue of a primitive way of thinking that we cannot shake off, it seems odd that otherwise perfectly modern minds, including a significant number of scientists, continue to hold religious beliefs. And that raises the second question: was the kind of understanding people sought when they did look to the divine the same kind of understanding that we now get from science, or is religion something completely different?

▶ Worse questions

These are not, however, the central questions usually found in introductions to the philosophy of religion, which take as their core the traditional arguments for the existence of God. There is the teleological argument, which claims that the universe shows the signs of having been designed with a purpose, pointing to a divine creator. Then there is the cosmological argument, which claims that since everything must have a cause sufficient to have produced it, the only cause powerful enough to explain the universe is a god. Also, there is the ontological argument, which argues that the very existence of the concept of 'the greatest being conceivable' means that such a being must exist: a non-existent greatest being being a contradiction in terms. If you're unlucky, you'll also get the moral argument: that the existence of moral laws proves the existence of a moral law-giver, which can only be God.

These arguments are interesting as puzzles to be solved, and for their historical and psychological impact. But philosophically and theologically, most would agree they are very weak. The teleological argument may once have appeared persuasive, but post Darwin, it should be obvious that what looks like design need be no such thing.

▲ Religion is more than a set of doctrines.

Against the cosmological argument, either everything needs a cause or it doesn't, and if it does, an uncaused God is no less puzzling than any non-divine first cause, such as a big bang. Against the ontological argument, if things can exist just because a concept such as perfection or greatness implies their existence, then the perfect goblin or greatest elf conceivable must exist too. As for the moral argument, it begs the question as to the status of moral laws: if they are human constructs or natural laws, then no god is required to explain their existence.

If these dismissals seem brusque, I make no apology. Plenty of ink has been spilled elsewhere running through the same old tired expositions, objections and replies. But very few philosophers are impressed by them, and if people of faith often find the logic persuasive, it is only because people are generally far too readily taken in by weak arguments that lead to conclusions they like. Very few believers base their faith on such arguments anyway. They take them as welcome intellectual support, but the foundations of their faith lie elsewhere.

A little, but not much more, can be said for the other two work-horses of the philosophy of religion: Pascal's Wager and the problem of evil. Pascal's Wager is the argument that you're better off believing in God than not because the risks of not believing and being wrong, such as ending up in Hell, are so severe, whereas the price for believing and being wrong is marginal: some wasted time being pious, compensated for by a great deal of comfort. The trouble is, of course, that you have to choose which god to worship and how, and when it comes to incurring God's wrath, worshipping a false idol is as risky, if not more so, than believing in none at all. Nor is it clear why God should reward you for believing in him only because you think it is prudent to do so.

The problem of evil is an argument against God's existence: how can there be so much suffering and pain in the world if it is ruled by an all-loving, all-powerful, all-knowing god? Only a god who didn't know, didn't care, or couldn't do anything about it would stand by and let it go on, and that is not the kind of god people believe in. Although I think this is a serious problem, if you think there are good reasons to believe in God and you accept that human understanding is limited, there is not much to be said against people who insist that God must have his reasons, unfathomable though they may be to us.

So I think it quite right that we should get these questions out of the way quickly and focus on what really matters: the question of what religion is and why it hasn't died in the secular, modern world.

▶ Religious impulses

One reason why the persistence of religion seems baffling to many is that they see it primarily as the belief that there is a god; there is a heaven; we have immortal, immaterial souls; God has inspired or dictated sacred texts; miracles have been performed and people have been brought back to life; and so on. If none of these things is literally true – and who in the twenty-first century could believe they are? – then religion is simply false and should be left behind, like other childish things.

This bafflement underestimates both how stupid and how clever people can be. Stupid because there are plenty of people who believe the most absurd, literal versions of their various religions, with no understanding of why they defy good sense. Clever because there are also people who believe some, if not all, of these traditional creeds, who understand full well where they seem to clash with modern science and history, but are able to reconcile these beliefs in ways that cannot be dismissed as simply ignorant. The mere existence of very intelligent believers is evidence that the persistence of religious belief cannot be put down simply to human stupidity.

But religion is about more than just a set of doctrines anyway. Religion can also be a practice, a way of life, a moral and social community. Rituals, texts and stories can serve as important elements of these without anyone having to believe that they are literal history, or alternatives to science. It is a basic mistake to think that religious texts and credos are making factual statements about the world. They are, rather, pointing to 'spiritual truths'.

But what exactly does this mean? Over recent decades, influenced by Wittgenstein, many have argued that religious language needs to be understood in a different way from scientific or historic language. Whatever a phrase like 'blood of Christ' means in the communion service, it does not indicate the presence of haemoglobin. Similarly, perhaps, 'eternal life' is not the literal continuation of individual humans after bodily death, but a way of living in connection with that which transcends the particulars of our own time and place and partakes in universal values. Even to talk of 'God' may be to talk not of a real entity but of an eternal principle of love.

This view is often called 'non-realist' religion, because it affirms the value and importance of religion while denying the real existence of gods, heavens and all things supernatural. It might be true that most religious believers do and have believed that God is real and that at least some of the claims of religion are literally true. But even if the person kneeling to pray in the church may believe that God is a kind of person, listening in, the reason why praying plays such an important part in his life could be that it provides a ritual of moral reflection and an orientation towards the eternal.

This might sound too subtle by half, but perhaps back in 325 AD, if you had asked the early Christians if the Nicene Creed asserted factual, historical claims or myths, they would not even have understood the question. There are reasons to think that the clear distinction between history and myth is a relatively recent one. Even today, believers are often unsure to what extent they think Bible stories really happened. Most don't think there was a great flood, but opinion is divided on whether Jesus really brought Lazarus back to life.

To many, such a reading of religion seems elitist and patronizing. It suggests that intellectuals understand what religion really is, while the masses get by on much more naïve assumptions. There are also concerns that if religion is reduced to a purely human creation, with no real, objective divine force to hold us to account, then our reasons for being religious in the first place are diminished, if not eradicated.

Death over dogma

People who claim doctrine is not important for religion can clearly overstate their case. Galileo was condemned as a heretic because of what he claimed about the real sun and the real earth, not because he chose the wrong metaphor. Today, many pernicious and false beliefs persist because people believe their religion demands they are true, when any objective observer should see they are false.

Nonetheless, it is also too simplistic to see the religious impulse as nothing more than a primitive attempt to understand the mechanics of the universe in supernatural terms. Rather, there are a number of religious impulses: for community, for meaning, for myths to live by, for rituals to give shape to life; for a way of thinking about that which transcends the here and now. To philosophize about religion fruitfully today is to think of these things. To get fixated on medieval arguments for God's existence or whether evolution is true or not is to focus on the worst that philosophy and religion have to say to us, not the best.

Who and What
Are We?

ALL THAT
MATTERS

On the face of it, the ability to look into a mirror and recognize that it is you looking back does not seem too remarkable. But as we now know, only a handful of creatures on this planet can do it: great apes, including human beings (but not until they are 18 months old), killer whales, bottlenose dolphins, elephants and European magpies.

This ability is considered to be significant because it is thought to demonstrate the presence of self-awareness. Few people now doubt that many, if not all, animals have some form of consciousness. A cat feels pain, a mouse smells food and so on. But as well as being subjects of experience, are any animals aware that they are also objects in the world? It is argued that those that pass the mirror test are. This capacity to understand ourselves as both subject and object, from the outside as well as the inside, is a vital part of what makes our philosophical nature possible. And such self-understanding is surely a prerequisite for knowing how we should live and what meaning, if any, humans can find in life.

So it is that philosophical anthropology has been one of the most fascinating and enduring strands of the subject. And, as usual, the story begins in Ancient Greece with Plato and Aristotle . . .

▶ In search of essence

'Haven't you realized that our soul is immortal and never destroyed?' So asks Socrates in Plato's *Republic,* and it's fascinating to speculate on how people during different times and ages would respond. Despite the supposed growth of scientific materialism in the West, a millennial BBC survey suggested that while only 26% of Britons believe in a personal God, 69% think we have a soul and 25% of us believe in reincarnation. These results match those of a Populus poll five years later, in which 71% expressed a belief in the existence of the soul and 53% in an afterlife.

One might then assume that belief in souls that can survive death is the default, common-sense position. But Glaucon's response to Socrates' question is to look at him 'with wonder' and say 'No, by God, I haven't. Are you really in a position to assert that?' Other characters in Plato's dialogues respond similarly. It seems that, among the educated classes at least, belief in an immortal soul was not at all widespread in Ancient Greece. But that is not to say they didn't believe in souls at all. In the *Phaedo*, Cebes says that people believe that 'after [the soul] has left the body it no longer exists anywhere, but that it is destroyed and dissolved on the day the man dies.'

Do Christians have souls?

The early Christian Church took as its model for the afterlife the bodily resurrection of Christ. The belief in souls that will live on independently of the body after death only entered Christian theology when it absorbed influences from Greek thought. So, although people tend to think of the immaterial soul as a Christian idea, many theologians reject it even today.

Cebes' statement may sound puzzling to modern ears. If we have a soul, then surely the whole point is that it is non-physical and survives death? That bafflement reflects the fact that the idea of soul that has prevailed in our culture is essentially the Platonic one contained within Socrates' question. But what is a soul if it is not immortal and immaterial? One answer is found in the work of Aristotle. On his view, soul (*psuchê*) is not a substance separate from matter. Rather, substance itself comprises both matter and form. By itself, matter is only inert potential. But when it takes on a certain organized form, such as in a plant or animal, it becomes part of the actuality of the substance. Any substance whose actuality involves life is said to have soul. Soul, then, is not a thing, but the capacities a living thing has which distinguish it from the non-living. The activities of souls form a hierarchy. First, there are the lower functions of self-nourishment, growth and decay that all living things, including plants, share. The higher functions of movement and rest are found only in the souls of animals. But the highest activity of the soul, intellect, is found only in humans.

Despite their disagreements, Aristotle and Plato both believe that human beings have some kind of *essence* that we need to live in accordance with. For Aristotle, this essence is to be a rational animal. This belief in essences, however, started to look vulnerable with the theory of evolution. Until then, it was not only possible, it seemed perfectly natural, to think of every species as being a unique kind with its own essential characteristics. But if we all evolved from a common ancestor, then no species has a fixed, immutable essence. The idea of essences as natural, found in both Plato and Aristotle, starts to look false.

Historically, there has also been a supernatural basis for the attribution of a special essence of humans. That is to say, if God made us, then he did so with a purpose. A decline in religious belief was bound to threaten this assumption, and no one did more to turn that threat into reality than Jean-Paul Sartre. Sartre argued that created objects, such as paperknives, have an essence that precedes their existence. That is to say, the whole reason they were brought into existence was to fulfil a function, and that function determines their nature. For humans, this is not true. With no god, we are just the products of blind, natural evolution. Thus, for us, 'existence precedes essence'. 'Essence', to the extent that we have it at all, is something for us to determine for ourselves.

However, before Sartre, even before Plato and Aristotle, another idea emerged which threatened our self-image even more deeply.

▶ On not having a self

Two and a half thousand years ago, under a pipal tree in Bodh Gaya, India, Siddhārtha Gautama attained enlightenment. At least, he thought he did, and so have the millions who have since followed his teachings, calling him the Buddha, the 'Awakened One'. And one idea he had was remarkably ahead of its time. In fact, it took more than two millennia for western philosophy to catch up, and today neuroscience seems to be supporting it.

That idea is captured in the Pali word *anattā*: not-self. That does not mean you or I do not exist. What it means is that there is no abiding, enduring self. You and I are simply a mixture of five *khandhas* ('aggregates'). We comprise our physical form and matter (*rūpa*); sensations which are pleasant, unpleasant or neutral (*vedanā*); perceptions of the five senses (*saññā*); thoughts, mental habits and opinions (*saṅkhāra*); and what is usually translated as consciousness or discernment (*viññāṇa*). Whether the list of *khandhas* provides the correct taxonomy or not, the principle is clear enough: we are the sum of our parts, mental and physical, and we do not exist separately from these parts. In many ways, this is similar to Aristotle's view: soul or self is not a separate thing but is simply what emerges when our parts work together.

That this view still seems radical today is perhaps surprising, as we have no problem thinking of everything else in the universe in this way. For instance, I might say water has two parts hydrogen and one part oxygen, but no one would think that this means that the oxygen and hydrogen atoms belong to some separate abiding thing, water. Rather, we understand that water just is the atoms, in the appropriate combination. In the same way, *anattā* says we are no more than the elements that make us up, suitably organized. This seems strange only because we have such a strong sense of unity that we feel as though we have some kind of stable core within us.

Meditation

The Buddha thought we could free ourselves of the illusion of a fixed, core self through the long practice of meditation. Interestingly, the Scottish philosopher David Hume came to pretty much the same conclusion and also thought introspection supported his view, although he seemed to think

a single careful look inside would do the trick. Just introspect for a while and try to capture the 'I' that is experiencing the world. Hume wagers all you'll find is this thought, that sensation, a memory, some kind of itch in your left leg and so on. You will find no self at the heart of this.

▲ Rembrandt, *Philosopher in Meditation*, 1632

The most common and strongest intuitive objection to this view is that you cannot even talk about thoughts and experiences without presupposing that someone is having them. So isn't it incoherent to argue that I can be aware that I have no awareness, or you can have the thought that there is no you having that thought? But this objection misses the point. The 'bundle theory', as it is sometimes called, does not deny that there is a you or an I. It simply denies that this you or I is separate from the sum of its parts. This is no more paradoxical than saying that an army can march across a battlefield, even though an army is nothing over and above an organized collection of troops.

Neuroscientists who are looking at how sense of self emerges in the brain are also discovering that there is no single centre of first-person consciousness in the brain, a kind of 'control room'. Rather, different parts of the brain are aware of different things to different degrees at different times. The sense we have of a single viewpoint, a single subject of experience, is actually a kind of fiction we unwittingly create to help keep our autobiographical memory simple.

Many advocates of the bundle view resort to language that suggests the self does not exist. For instance, the psychologist Bruce Hood calls his book *The Self Illusion* and the philosopher Thomas Metzinger uses the phrase 'myth of the self' in the subtitle of his book *The Ego Tunnel*. In one sense this is right, because the sense we have of a permanent, abiding self is an illusion. But take away 'permanent, abiding' and there is still a self. If the self is not real, then neither are armies nor water.

Not everyone accepts the bundle theory, of course. A few still believe in a separate, immaterial soul, though their numbers are very small in philosophy and virtually zero in neuroscience. Even many who do not fully embrace the bundle theory accept that we are mortal, changeable creatures without a separate, abiding self that exists unchanged throughout life and perhaps after it too. That's a major fact to get your head around and, as we'll see later, must surely inform our views about how we should live and what meaning there is in life.

The Value of Art

ALL THAT
MATTERS

Like most people lucky enough to have travelled, I've been to some of the world's great art galleries, such as the Prado in Madrid, the Uffizi in Florence and New York's Met. But perhaps the most affecting was a small, dark space in Asturias, northern Spain. La Cueva de Tito Bustillo, in the quiet fishing village of Ribadesella, contains none of the works of the great masters. On show are original cave paintings from the palaeolithic era, created between 22,000 and 10,000 BCE.

But why did those early humans create these works? It is tempting to offer a purely anthropological answer: perhaps the images served some religious or ceremonial function. When you actually see the images, however, it becomes hard to believe that this is the whole story. There is pure aesthetic merit in many of these works, independent of any function they might have had.

Given the age of these images and others like them around the world, it seems likely that art predates philosophy, and so people produced art before they philosophized about it. But it also seems likely that when human beings started thinking about where value came from and how we ought to live, the question of what art was and why it mattered would have begun to get a grip on them. And it has proved to be an enduring and frustrating question, in part because there are too many different answers.

▶ What is art?

Sometimes it seems that contemporary art isn't doing its job unless it provokes the question, 'But is it art?' I'm not sure the question is worth asking. It seems to

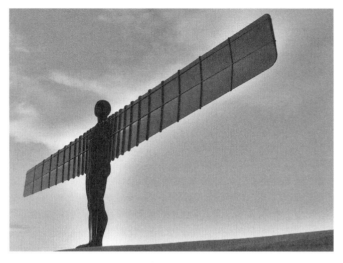

▲ Antony Gormley's *Angel of the North*, 1998

me that the line between art and not-art is never going to be a sharp one. Worse, as the various art forms – poetry, drama, sculpture, painting, fiction, dance, etc. – are so different, I'm not sure why we should expect to be able to come up with a single definition that can capture their variety. Art seems to be a paradigmatic example of a Wittgensteinian 'family resemblance' concept. Try to specify the necessary and sufficient condition for something qualifying as art and you'll always find an exception to your criteria. If philosophy were to admit defeat in its search for some immutable essence of art, it is hardly through lack of trying. Arguably, we have very good reasons for thinking that this has been one of the biggest wild goose chases in the history of ideas.

Perhaps this is why the institutional theory of art, proposed by Arthur C Danto in 1964, has become so popular. In summary form, it sounds crude, almost anti-philosophical: something is a work of art if the 'artworld' says it is. 'Art' is like any number of concepts, the application of which depends purely on contingent social facts. There is no natural distinction, for instance, between what is legal and illegal. Legal is what the law says it is. Similarly, there is no Platonic form of fashion. What is fashionable is a combination of what people buy and what the fashion world decrees.

In any case, perhaps what matters more than whether or not something is art is whether or not it is any good. If I were to try to create a work of art, I would not take much comfort from being told that it is indeed art, but it's terrible. So rather than thinking about the essence of art, would we not be better to think about the value of art?

▶ Why value art?

Sometimes we value art for very personal reasons: a piece of music is tied to a particular memory; a painting is by a deceased friend; a film's plot-line resonates with our own lives. Philosophical aesthetics, however, concerns itself with reasons why anyone would – or perhaps even should – appreciate a work of art. I think these fall into six general categories.

The first, and most obvious, is that art gives us pleasure, which most aestheticians argue is of a special kind. Kant, for instance, claimed that aesthetic pleasure is 'disinterested', meaning that it is not mixed up with other desires or practical needs. A meal may be delicious, for example, but it also provides fuel and sates hunger. A car may be beautiful but it also is a way of getting from A to B, and confers status on its owner. To enjoy art properly, Kant believed we had to appreciate it without any concern for any practical advantage it might give us. In contrast, art critic Ananda Coomaraswamy uses an Indian word that is tricky to translate – *rasa* – to describe the particular spiritual rather than sensory pleasure of art. In their different ways, both Kant and Coomaraswamy tried to capture the sense we have that art gives us a higher kind of pleasure than what we get from food, sex or soccer.

Higher pleasure?

Many find the idea that art produces a higher form of pleasure intuitively compelling. But there is also a suspicion that attempts to claim a higher pleasure for art are simply a snobbish way to justify elitist preferences. According to Jeremy Bentham, for example, pleasure is pleasure, whether it is derived from a simple game such as push-pin or from high art such as poetry.

A second tradition identifies beauty as the central value in art. For the critic Clive Bell, this beauty is found in its 'significant form', the way in which the elements of the artwork harmoniously combine. This results in a purely aesthetic kind of appreciation that has nothing to do with what the work might represent or mean. So, for example, the significant form of Picasso's cubist painting *Musiciens aux masques* ('Musicians with Masks') is a function of the different lines, patterns, colours and so on. The fact that it actually represents three musicians in some way is – or should be – irrelevant to our appreciation of it. While this may seem credible in this example, it is harder to see how the subject matter of, say, the ceiling of the Sistine Chapel, can be ignored when assessing its aesthetic merit.

Both these accounts focus on the artwork and the reaction it provokes in us. A third tradition moves the focus back to the artist herself, locating value in the success an artwork has in conveying the feelings of the artist. However, there is a strong counterargument that works of art, once created, take on a life of their own and have to be assessed on their own merits. The original intentions or feelings of their creators are both irrelevant and ultimately unknowable anyway. Hence, to think that they matter to the value or meaning of the work is to commit what WK Wimsatt and Monroe Beardsley called the 'intentional fallacy'.

If they are right, then Tolstoy is an example of a thinker who made this mistake. He argued that good art is infectious, and that this is primarily down to the sincerity of the artist and her ability to convey her feelings. However, he also thought that great art infected us only with good, noble feelings. Hence, Tolstoy became virtually the only person in history to have considered many of his didactic, Christian short stories to be superior to *War and Peace* or *Anna Karenina*.

Tolstoy is thus associated with a fourth set of criteria for valuing art: the idea that art is educative in some way. For Tolstoy, this education is direct, through the moral lessons derived from drama and fiction. Others have argued that art educates us indirectly, by getting us to focus on what is true and good. This is exemplified by the aesthetics of Schiller. Art offers us a space of 'creative play' that helps us to make sense of ourselves and the world. So, for instance, he wrote, 'By beauty the sensuous man is led to form and to thought; by beauty the spiritual man is brought back to matter and restored to the world of sense.'

A fifth tradition also sees in art an ability to convey truths, this time about the real nature of the world. Again, we see this manifest in various different forms. For Schopenhauer, the fundamental force driving everything in the universe is what he called 'will': a blind, senseless striving for survival, replication and power. Art was our means of apprehending this but also of temporarily escaping its power. For Dewey, art is what enables us to experience the fundamental unity of reality, which the hubbub of normal life separates us from. Both Pythagoras and Hsun Tzu thought that music in particular reflected the divine harmony of the universe.

I would say there is also a sixth tradition, but it is actually hardly visible in the canon of western philosophical aesthetics. It is, however, evident in a common dismissive reaction to much contemporary art: 'I could have done that.' People often have a strong sense that great art requires exceptional skill and talent, and that part of what impresses us is being elevated by the experience of what we could never experience if left purely to ourselves. Perhaps in this sense the value of art is that it enables us to transcend our own limitations by connecting with humanity's highest creative achievements.

▶ Inconclusion

I find aesthetics to be at the same time one of the most interesting and one of the most pointless branches of philosophy. Interesting because it helps us to attend to the various ways in which art matters; pointless because art is too varied for there to be any hope of defining what it is or what gives it value. Nevertheless, much of philosophy's value derives not from its ability to deliver neat answers, but in its power to make us attend to what matters, what we might otherwise have missed. If, at best, aesthetics can come up with a menu of possibilities, some of which apply to some works of art, some of which to others, that is not a worthless achievement.

However, I also have another worry, one that I am often reminded of when I read curators' captions in art galleries. It seems to me that much of what is valuable about art is not translatable into non-artistic means of expression, such as prose writing or speech. Often I feel the less said about some art the better, and the more we try to sum up its 'meaning' in words, the more we distance ourselves from what is distinctive about it as an aesthetic experience. We should perhaps just let art be art, and philosophy be philosophy.

9

States and Nature

ALL THAT
MATTERS

You could get by in life without giving the value of art much thought, but some other normative concerns are more urgent and unavoidable. Take the central question of politics: how should we live together? This question is clearly as important today as it has ever been. Few would be so complacent as to suggest that developed western democracies have got it all right, and their systems differ in important ways anyway. In the aftermath of 2011's Arab Spring, many Middle Eastern nations looked for democratic models of government that suited their own tribal and religious traditions. As other countries develop, they are looking for their own models of governance, such as 'capitalism with Chinese characteristics'.

More profoundly, the nature of the globalized world is changing and there are real question marks over how fit the established nation-state model is to deal with a vastly interconnected planet. National governments are ceding power to transnational bodies such as the European Union and African Union and transnational treaties such as the North American Free Trade Area.

Politics is still very much a work in progress, which is why the philosophical work already done provides a valuable resource. Inevitably, some of the earliest and most enduring contributions to that stockpile came from the pens of the two giants of Greek philosophy: Plato and Aristotle.

▶ Fit for purpose

As usual, Plato and Aristotle approach the question of how the state should be organized in two different ways.

Plato's strategy is to construct an ideal, hypothetical state: the eponymous *Republic* of his most famous dialogue. Aristotle, in contrast, surveys existing states, wanting to make sure that his prescription is rooted in real experience.

This is much more than a mere methodological difference. It has often been argued that the Platonic approach is disastrous in the real world. Look at the worst political regimes in modern history and you'll find that they almost all tried to shoehorn established societies into a supposedly more perfect mould, created without thought to the particulars of history and context. 'Ordering society along more rational lines' sounds so reasonable, but, in practice, it has often meant tearing the existing fabric of society so much that it is destroyed in the process. The most extreme expression of this idea came with Pol Pot's attempt to take Cambodia to a 'year zero', rebuilding the country from scratch. The result was one of the most barbaric regimes in history, which cost the lives of one in five of the population.

Looked at in that light, it might seem much better to go with, rather than against, the grain of existing structures and traditions. This is one of the strongest arguments for Conservatism. That doesn't mean rejecting all major reforms: starting from where we are now does not mean refusing to stray too far from it. So although there is small-c conservatism in the Aristotelian approach, it needn't always end up being the capitalized variety.

Despite their different approaches, both Plato and Aristotle favoured rule by an elite and were suspicious of democracy. For Plato, the best rulers would be philosophers, since they know what is good and they have no desire for power, and so would not be corrupted by holding it. By forcing them to become 'philosopher kings', we would avoid the problem inherent in politics: that people who seek power are precisely those we wouldn't want to hold it. For Aristotle too, since 'the good life . . . is the chief aim of society, both collectively for all its members and individually', it made no sense to grant everyone the same right to rule, irrespective of how well they can contribute to this end.

Although most people can sympathize with this, we are generally less inclined than Plato and Aristotle to believe that there is indeed a trustworthy, wise elite to whom we can entrust power, and, even if there were, we would not know how to identify it. However, the case against democracy is not just that the people are ignorant. For Aristotle, the key was that democracy undermines the rule of law. The best society creates the right laws and then we all live under them. In the worst societies, the interests and wishes of an individual (tyranny), group (oligarchy) or the people (democracy) take precedence over the law. Politics becomes a way of expressing the will of whoever holds power, when it should be about upholding the principles of justice that apply to all.

These three decadent forms of government also have another flaw in common. To put it in the language of a later political paradigm, they pit the interests of one class over another. Tyranny pits the ruler against his subjects; oligarchy the powerful elite against the rest of society; and democracy the majority against the minority.

Interestingly, however, Aristotle believes there is a good form of government paired to each of the three bad ones. In contrast to tyranny, proper 'kingship' is the good rule of one over all. Aristocracy, not oligarchy, is the right model for rule of a few over the many. And polity, not democracy, is how the many should rule themselves. Of the three, however, he preferred rule by the few over rule by the many because he believed rulers should be the people best able to further the goals of the state, and that meant the best, most virtuous persons: *aristoi*.

Was Aristotle aristocratic?

To call Aristotle's political philosophy 'aristocratic' is technically correct but misleading, as today we associate that word with people who have inherited status and wealth, not the real great and the good of society. Aristotle's *aristoi* were the people genuinely best qualified to govern, not just those of noble birth.

For Plato and Aristotle, the most pressing question was what kind of state was best. However, in later centuries, political philosophers took the question one stage further and asked, 'What justifies the existence of a state at all?'

▶ Justifying the state

When discussing how the state should be organized, we tend to take it for granted that there needs to be one. Anarchist writers such as Mikhail Bakunin have

▲ Living in a civil state requires us to give up some of our individual liberties.

questioned this. One reason why few now take them seriously might have something to do with the fact that 'anarchy' has become synonymous with chaos in popular parlance, even though it really simply means lack of ruler or sovereign – *archê* in Greek. But even discounting this distorting linguistic accident, few believe that we could do without states in the massively populated, complex world we live in today. Nevertheless, the anarchist offers an important challenge: given that the existence of a state always requires citizens to give up some power over their own lives, we need to justify the state in order to justify those deprivations of liberty. It's not good enough simply to say the state is a practical necessity, because that doesn't tell us what kind of state we need.

One way in which a number of thinkers have addressed this problem is to imagine we are bound by a hypothetical 'social contract'. The idea is that we all implicitly sign up to a deal by which we give up certain individual freedoms in exchange for the benefits and protections offered by a civil state. Given that no such real contract exists and no one has ever consciously signed it, we need to ask, 'What are its terms and why are we obliged to honour them?' And the answer to both questions has been given by considering the alternative: life in a 'state of nature'.

Thomas Hobbes was one of the most famous philosophers to argue in this way. As he memorably put it, outside of a civilized society, the natural state would be 'a war of every man, against every man' and 'the life of man, solitary, poor, nasty, brutish, and short'. For Jean-Jacques Rousseau, however, our natural state is one of liberty. Prior to the construction of societies, a human was a 'noble savage' who was naturally good. The problem is other people. We have to get along with them, keep the peace with them and share limited resources with them. From this springs all human vice: greed, acquisitiveness, envy, competition, deceit and so on. Rousseau's vision of the state of nature may sound hopelessly romantic, but his explanation of why we can no longer live in it comes across as misanthropic.

So whereas Hobbes imagined the state of nature to be a horror we must escape, for Rousseau it is an Eden we cannot re-enter. The upshot for both is, however, very similar. For Hobbes, the necessity of escaping the barbarous state of nature requires us to make a deal with the human beings we would otherwise be fighting. In effect, we all say, 'I authorize and give up my right of governing, to this man, or to this assembly of men, on this condition, that thou give up thy right to him, and authorize all his actions in like manner.' For that 'man' or 'assembly of men' to be able to do the job, they need absolute power. Hence, the state or commonwealth that comes into existence must be one which has absolute power to which all must defer. Hobbes called this Leviathan.

For Rousseau, we implicitly do a deal not to give up our freedoms to a third party, but to pool our powers over ourselves. So, rather than each following an individual will, we all come together and follow the general will. Hence, the terms of Rousseau's social contract are that 'Each one of us puts into the community his person and all his powers under the supreme direction of the general will; and as a body, we incorporate every member as an indivisible part of the whole.' Although this is in many ways fundamentally different from Hobbes' conception, Rousseau himself seemed to accept that the practical result was very similar. For Hobbes, we are all subjects of the omnipotent Leviathan; for Rousseau, 'Man was born free, and he is everywhere in chains.'

One of the main problems of social contract theories is what to do about people who reject its terms. Rousseau's answer is that the whole point of pooling our liberty is that, in effect, our will is subsumed under the general will. So if we want something different from what the populace as a whole wants, then that merely shows we have made a mistake as to what the general will is. As democracy is having your say, not getting your way, there is no contradiction in having to obey laws you neither voted for nor agree with.

This argument, however, still rests on the assumption that you have indeed pooled sovereignty with others. But what if you don't want even to do that? It seems we are given no choice whether we accept the terms of the social contract or not, but the whole idea of a contract makes no sense if you have no option but to sign it. Rousseau's solution to this problem is to insist that 'residence implies consent: to inhabit the territory is to submit to the sovereign'. However, the idea that people can move elsewhere if they don't like their political system is unrealistic.

Despite their weaknesses, the arguments of Hobbes and Rousseau contain within them several insights which are still relevant and true today. Whatever the imperfections of nation states, we have no choice but to come together, giving up some individual freedoms in return for protection against the violent or exploitative actions of others. The problems in Hobbes and Rousseau merely alert us to what are the ongoing problems with any state: it constantly needs to justify the freedoms it denies its citizens and show that it is giving them real benefits in return. The metaphor of the contract may be misleading, but the *quid pro quo* it implies is at the heart of any justification for a state. And, as we have seen, when citizens do believe that their rulers are taking too much freedom and not delivering in return, they have a tendency to turf them out, through either the ballot box or revolution.

However we ought to live together, most would accept that it leaves a lot of room for each of us to decide how to live our individual lives. Prior to politics, there is ethics.

Doing Right and Doing Well

What does the phrase 'the good life' evoke in your imagination? Do you think of sunning yourself on the deck of a yacht, glass of champagne in hand? Or do you rather imagine an ascetic monk, tending to the needs of the poor? Or are you part of the generation of Britons who immediately think of the popular sitcom of the same name, in which a suburban couple try to escape the rat race by becoming self-sufficient? Strange though it may sound, from a philosophical point of view, it's the television show that has the most helpful associations.

When we think of 'good' in relation to human life, we often think of doing well: what it means for your life to be good for you. This has been the subject of much research in recent years in the field of positive psychology, and there are now studies to support common-sense ideas that people's self-reported life satisfaction is usually most affected by health, sufficient wealth, good relationships and satisfying work. But in addition to doing well, we also have a sense that we ought to do right. It matters not only that your life *feels* good, but that you *do* good. A good life in this sense is honest, altruistic and caring.

In *The Good Life,* doing right and doing well are not unrelated. Although the main characters, Tom and Barbara, embrace relative austerity, living in this way makes them happier than commuting to the office. They do well by doing right, even though that requires sacrifice and less overt self-concern. Whatever contentment they find arises naturally from their form of life, not because they pursue happiness directly.

Does this optimistic view of the relationship between doing right and doing good hold up in the real world? I would suggest this is the central question of philosophical ethics. It hasn't always looked that way, but it was evident back at the birth of the subject.

▶ Flourishing

When we think of doing good today, we do so through the spectacles of centuries of Christian influence on our culture. There are rules about what we should do and, perhaps even more importantly, what we should not do: of the ten commandments, eight are prohibitions. Our inherited moral code is thus a kind of quasi-legal code, in which God is legislator, law enforcer and judge. Theologically, this summary is somewhat naïve, but it does describe the implicit assumptions about morality made by our inherited framework of Bible-based morality.

So it may come as a surprise to read Ancient Greek ethics and find Aristotle talking about how many friends we should have, and Plato about whether or not it is possible for the good man to be harmed by misfortune. These would appear to be beside the point. Jesus may have implored us to love our neighbours but he didn't give advice on how to manage close personal friendships, and his crucifixion was nothing to do with bad luck.

The strangeness is an indicator of how our thinking about good has shifted from ethics to morality. Surprisingly, perhaps, there is no simple, widely agreed way of distinguishing between these two terms. However, Kwame Anthony Appiah seems to get close to the nub of it when he suggests that morality concerns only one's relationship to others, whereas ethics is about what it means for a person to live a good life in a wider sense. This fits in with my understanding of the distinction, which is that morality is about the actions we need to do or avoid, or the rules we need to follow, in order to do right by other people, whereas ethics is about what we need to do in order to flourish ourselves.

In that sense, when we read the likes of Plato and Aristotle, we arguably do not read moral philosophy at all. Their central question was the ethical one and morality did not exist as a distinct subject. So, for example, Plato could take seriously the suggestion that 'justice is nothing other than the advantage of the stronger', because there was no assumption that ethics must involve moral obligations to others. When Plato and others did conclude that the ethical life requires following what we would now think of as moral rules, they did so because they thought doing wrong is bad for you and made it impossible for you to flourish.

That word is crucial. You will often read that Aristotle claimed happiness was the highest human good, but the word he used was not happiness but *eudaimonia*, usually translated as flourishing. Shakespeare's Hamlet was right when he said 'one may smile, and smile, and be a villain', and he could have added that a villain may laugh and be rich too. When we decide to live virtuously rather than viciously, we do so not because we think it will make us more cheerful, but because we recognize that villainy makes us less than fully human. There are good reasons why it is both common and apt to describe the lives of the most wicked and violent as sub-human. To set aside thought for others and to live purely for what provides material and hedonic advantage is to live as a cunning animal, not a wise person. That is why many judge that it really is 'better to die as men than live as beasts'.

Hence, thinking ethically is radically and importantly different to thinking morally, even though both usually end up delivering a similar set of prescriptions. Now that fewer and fewer people accept religious authority as the source of morality, it is perhaps vitally important that we rediscover this. Otherwise, we are left with no compelling reasons why we should not just look after number one and exploit others if we get the chance.

▶ Why be good?

In theory, it sounds wonderful that ethics and morality form such a natural alliance. But doesn't this sound a little too good to be true? Perhaps we can accept that doing good and doing well do not *always* coincide, just as long as we have good reason to suppose they *usually* do. There is an old legal adage that 'hard cases make for bad law' and, similarly, what happens unusually could be a bad guide for how to live usually. But what reasons do we have to think that doing right is *generally* part of doing well? For Aristotle, and to some extent Plato too, the answer was that everything should live according to its nature, which for us means living in accordance with our higher, intellectual capacities. This line of argument is less persuasive today, because, to the extent that we have a natural essence, it is merely the product of evolution, and that tells us nothing about whether we should act on it or try to counteract it. Too often it is assumed that 'it's natural' functions as a justification, when really it is just a description. It may be natural, for example, to prioritize your family over strangers, but for a public official to do this while at work would be grossly wrong.

Getting away with murder

In Woody Allen's *Crimes and Misdemeanors,* the protagonist, played by Martin Landau, has his lover murdered and is plagued with guilt, convinced that at some point he will have to pay for his sin. But, as he puts it himself using the third person, 'one morning, he awakens. The sun is shining, his family is around him and, mysteriously, the crisis has lifted. He takes his family on a vacation to Europe and as the months pass, he finds he's not punished. In fact, he prospers.' Without a God to even the score, sometimes people literally get away with murder, while others lose everything through no fault of their own.

Nevertheless, there is a way in which understanding human nature might help to close the gap between ethics and morality. The central idea is one that emerged in eighteenth-century Scotland, in the writings of Adam Smith, Francis Hutcheson and David Hume.

Although each of these thinkers differed, all agreed that sympathy or empathy was at the heart of morality. Empathy enables us to inhabit the point of view of another and to have a sense of what it means for them to suffer, be harmed or to thrive. This, rather than rational argument, both enables us to take the interests of others into account and motivates us to do something about it. 'How selfish soever man may be supposed,' wrote Smith, 'there are evidently some principles in his nature, which

▲ Sympathy is at the heart of morality

interest him in the fortunes of others, and render their happiness necessary to him, though he derives nothing from it, except the pleasure of seeing it.'

Clearly there is some truth in this. But still there is the worry that this only tells us what is the case, not what ought to be the case. And it was Hume himself who drew our attention to the intellectual sleight of hand by which people start describing 'is' and then slide into prescribing 'ought'. Was Hume therefore guilty of the committing the same mistake he had spotted in others?

The answer to this is to be found in another of Hume's memorable quotes: 'Reason is, and ought only to be, the slave of the passions.' This puts into colourful terms the insight that because you can never derive an 'is' from an 'ought', and because reason – meaning rationality – must stick with the facts of what is, reason alone could never tell you what you ought to do or want to do.

That is not to say rationality has no role to play in practical or ethical reasoning. Just as long as you have a goal or value, rational thought can help you work out whether it is coherent, whether it fits with other values, and how to achieve it. So, for instance, if you want to avoid causing unnecessary pain to others, reason can help you figure out what sort of living things you have to watch out for and how your actions will affect their welfare. But as to why you should ultimately care about the pain of others, reason is silent.

One way to understand this is to think about the distinction between reason (rationality) and reasons (motivations or justifications). In Hume's view, reason does not provide us with reasons. So the fact that reasons are provided by moral sentiment rather than logic does not betray some awful shortcoming of ethics. It is simply the inevitable result of the inability of reason to provide reasons. Moral feelings can be defeated only by other feelings – perhaps amoral or immoral ones – not rational arguments. And so, ultimately, at bedrock, ethics does boil down to a judgement: is it better to value the lives, feelings and projects of others or not?

There is no doubt that many, if not most, find this approach to ethics – usually called emotivism – unsatisfactory. My own view is tough: life is often unsatisfactory, and in this case I can't see how it could be any other way. Others, however, think they can.

▶ Doing your duty

There is a tradition in philosophy which insists that reason can provide reasons to act morally. It can do this because reason demands consistency, and consistency turns out to demand morality.

The general form of arguments to this effect is to start by considering what you think you ought to do, or are allowed to do. At this stage, morality need not be presumed. You might think you can do anything you want, or that you ought to do what is in your own best interests, irrespective of its effects on others.

The next stage is the critical one. Having decided that you are permitted to do something, does that mean that others in relevantly similar circumstances are also permitted to do the same? It would seem irrational to conclude that they are not. You cannot say something is true of one thing but not of another unless there is a relevant difference. For instance, one person but not another might be allowed on a theme park ride, because the second is too heavy for the safety regulations or because the first person took the last place. We might also allow some people to do things that others may not on the grounds of age: infants can't vote, adults can. But it would simply be irrational to allow some adults but not others to vote in the absence of a relevant difference between them which could be rationally explained.

So it appears to be a demand of reason that, if you think you are permitted to do something, you must allow that others are allowed to do it too, all other things being equal. This is called the principle of universalizability. This principle also implies a limit on what you can do: you cannot assert that you are entitled to do something if it is not possible to allow others to do the same. To take a very clear example, if I think I am free to murder whoever I want, I must accept that others are justified in doing the same. But given that I don't want to be murdered, I can't universalize the rule 'everyone should be free to kill whoever they want'. And given that you can only follow principles that are universalizable, you must conclude that you cannot kill whoever you want either.

So, by the use of reason alone it seems we have arrived at a fundamental moral law. In general form if not in detail, this is the line of reasoning that led the most famous proponent of this kind of view, Immanuel Kant, to formulate this fundamental principle as the 'categorical imperative': 'act only in accordance with that maxim through which you can at the same time will that it become a universal law'.

It's a compelling argument, but does it succeed in refuting Hume's claim that an ought can never follow from an is? It's not clear that it does. The Kantian line of argument appears to be purely rational only because the moral assumptions on which it rests seem so obvious that they don't need justifying. But they are still assumptions; namely, that we are morally bound by the demands of rational consistency, or that we ought not to endorse general rules that lead to more death or violence. These are certainly principles that I would hope we would endorse, but Hume's retort would be that it is not logic but feeling that persuades us that inconsistency or suffering is bad.

Despite their differences, perhaps the Kantian and Humean approaches both distinguish too sharply between facts on the one hand and feelings and values on the other. Kant is wrong to think we can derive values from reason as he misses the fact that the values are already there when reason gets to work, whereas Hume believes we cannot derive values from reason because his idea of reason is artificially isolated from moral sentiment. Reason's job is not to generate values from thin air, but to untangle and interrogate the values that are deeply embedded in how we think.

▶ A fine mess

Sometimes a book has such a good title I don't want to ruin things by actually reading it. Such is the case of *Messy Morality* by C A J Coady. Ethics is an untidy business and I believe the biggest mistake made by philosophers has been to try to clear it up too much. The way I see it, all of the great moral philosophers have been right in what they have identified as being important in ethics, but wrong in trying to make that factor the bedrock upon which all moral reasoning stands. Kant rightly saw that rational universalizability was important, but failed to see that reason takes us only so far. Hume was right to see that moral sentiment is indispensable, but wrong to downplay the role of reason in regulating and educating it. Aristotle was right to see character and habit as vital to making us good people, but perhaps not aware enough of the need for a decent number of clear rules that apply to all. Utilitarians were right to point out that the moral significance of actions has to attend to their consequences, but were wrong to make consequences the be-all and end-all, and also often wrong in seeing only certain types of consequences – most commonly happiness and the avoidance of suffering – as important.

As with aesthetics, the real value of moral philosophy might be to do with attention. I don't think moral philosophy will ever succeed in coming up with a system or principle that can serve as the basis of all morality. But it can help us to attend to those areas of our lives, our selves and our ways of reasoning that can help us to develop clearer moral vision. Moral progress is made when we see the mess of real life more clearly. Having done so, we can tidy it up a bit, but there will always be a strong element of just working with it.

The Meaning of Life

In the fable which opened this book, the journey into the most abstract reaches of philosophy started with the first human being who didn't just get on with existing, but asked why she should do so. The traditional myth about the birth of philosophy, however, starts not with the threat of despair, but with the promise of wonder. Aristotle said, 'It was their wonder, astonishment, that first led men to philosophise and still leads them', while Plato wrote 'philosophy begins in wonder'.

To say philosophy begins with wonder suggests a kind of delight, a burning curiosity that excites and stirs us. Philosophy turns on a light which we use to peer more closely and deeply into the world and to discover unimagined richness and interest in it. If, however, philosophy begins with wondering what the point of life is, then it is more like a cloud passing over us than the sun coming out. There is something Eden-like about this version of the story. Before philosophy, we were innocent, simply getting on with living. In place of the tree of knowledge is the tree of *sophia*, wisdom and, by eating its fruit, we achieve knowledge of the difference not between good and evil, but between the meaningful and the meaningless. The catch is that the first bite only opens our eyes to the fact that there is a difference. Once we start asking what the point of life is, however, we face the constant threat that the answer might be that there is none.

It is futile to ask which of the two accounts of the root of the philosophical impulse is true, not only because there is no historical or biographical fact of the matter, but because not everyone comes to philosophy for the same reason. Some approach it with starry-eyed wonder, whereas others come with furrowed brows, troubled by the seeming nonsensicalness of the universe.

What good would it have done such a seeker to have taken the journey from questions about the value and nature of her own life, through to thoughts about politics and art, to attempts to understand the nature of science, mind and language, right to the more abstract issues of the nature of truth and knowledge and the fundamental structure of reality? Let us imagine such a seeker – call her Sophia. Having travelled so far from issues of immediate concern to her life, will she be able to make more sense of her own existential questions when she turns her mind inward again?

Given that so many issues in philosophy are inconclusive, you might doubt that she would. However, although philosophers are far from unanimous in their thinking, on many issues there is a clear majority view, and even where there is a disagreement, in a strange way, that can also point to a deeper consensus. This is more than just a hunch. A few years ago, two philosophers conducted a survey of academic philosophers to find out what they believed. I want to suggest that if Sophia came to the same conclusions as the average contemporary philosopher, she would have learned enough to help her figure out what the point of living is. (The figures quoted are the percentage of philosophers who agree with the view expressed.)

Perhaps the first and most important thing to note is that the two dead philosophers with whom Sophia most identifies are Hume and Aristotle. I was personally delighted to discover this because the pair are my own philosophical heroes. What I find wonderful about them is that both manage the delicate balance between being as rigorous and precise as possible while accepting the limitations of human thought and being prepared to accept ambiguity, uncertainty and vagueness where necessary. Hume captures the spirit of this in his phrase 'mitigated scepticism'. Hume was opposed to the kind of 'excessive scepticism' which suspends all judgement and holds everything to be unknowable. But he did maintain that 'there is a degree of doubt, and caution, and modesty, which, in all kinds of scrutiny and decision, ought for ever to accompany a just reasoner'.

The perils of wonder

Although wonder is often thought to be central to philosophy, Hume argued that too much of it can actually lead us away from sound reasoning to flights of fancy. 'The imagination of man is naturally sublime,' he wrote, 'delighted with whatever is remote and extraordinary, and running, without control, into the most distant parts of space and time.'

So before we even think about what specific conclusions Sophia comes to, we already know that she has learned a great deal about what we might call the intellectual virtues of rigour, subtlety and mitigated scepticism. It is perhaps therefore not surprising to discover that although Sophia may have doubts about what precisely we can know about the external world, she believes that it really exists (82%) and that science does not merely construct models, but can tell us about how the universe really works (75%). Looking out into this universe she concludes that there is no god who created it or who controls it (73%). Nevertheless, she still believes that moral values are real (66%) and is more inclined to believe that aesthetic judgements can be objective (41%) than she is to think they are merely in the eye of the beholder (34%). When it comes to deciding which moral theory to adopt, however, she cannot make up her mind between the deontological approach of Kant (26%), consequentialism (24%) or Aristotelian virtue ethics (18%).

Looking back into herself, she concludes that her mind is a physical thing (56%) and that although she is free to act according to her own nature and decisions, there is a sense in which all of her choices are the effects of prior events and that, at any given time, she could not have done otherwise (59%).

Having reached these conclusions, what, finally, does Sophia think when she considers the question that started all this off: what is the meaning of life? First and foremost, she will have learned that the question itself needs questioning. What is the meaning of 'meaning' here? A natural answer is 'purpose' or 'point'. The meaning of life is that to which it is all leading: salvation or enlightenment, perhaps. But Sophia is an atheist who believes that when her physical body dies so will her mind. So if that is what is meant by meaning, life has none.

There is, however, another way of understanding meaning. When we ask what the point of living is, we are really asking where its value lies. The fact that its value is not to be found in some transcendent realm or in a life to come does not bother Sophia, because she has adopted Hume and Aristotle's concern with worldly reality, not heavenly dreams or speculations. 'A correct Judgement,' wrote Hume, avoids 'all distant and high enquiries, confines itself to common life, and to such subjects as fall under daily practice and experience; leaving the more sublime topics to the embellishment of poets and orators, or to the arts of priests and politicians.' It is therefore fitting to seek the meaning *of* life *in* life, and not in something else. If this seems a modest enterprise, it is only because we have come to accept too readily the immodest vanity of those who believe that our value and dignity as human beings derives from some divine sanction.

In Aristotle, as well as in many other Ancient Greek thinkers, you find next to nothing on what most people would recognize as the question of life's meaning. In its place is rather a lot on how to live. But this is actually the same question framed in a particular way. If you know how we should live you know what it means for a human life to achieve its highest value, to be worth living. If you know that, you have located 'the meaning of life' in arguably the only way that makes sense.

There is one more way, however, in which we need to parse 'the meaning of life' if we are to locate it: we must drop the definite article. 'The' meaning of life does not exist, if by that we mean a single source of value that makes life worth living. As Sophia's uncertainty about moral and political values shows, it is not at all clear that one value or even one set of values stands out as the right one for all people at all times. For sure, there are some things which seem to be especially important for a good, meaningful life. Doing well generally requires doing right, so we need to have a good moral sense. Pain and suffering are unavoidable but we have every reason to minimize them. Beyond that, however, it seems there is a long list of potential ingredients of a good life, and each person can concoct his or her own recipe in an attempt to create one for him- or herself. That is not to say anything goes. As with cookery, many things either never make good ingredients or can only be used sparingly, to provide spice or aid the process. That's why no one can ever say 'this is *the* meaning of life' and produce a final, clear answer for everyone.

One important consequence of this is that the meaning of life is not some kind of answer, which, once learned, is forever possessed. For life to stay meaningful it must continue to contain things of value, and that is an ongoing work in progress. Meaning can vanish: what we once found gave us a reason to exist we can lose or tire of. There is an old saying that life is a journey, not a destination, and the same is true of life's meaning.

And that is the meaning of life.

I know from experience that many people are not satisfied by this. Take the contemporary philosopher John Cottingham. He suggests that a meaningful life requires achievement (a form of doing well) and virtue (doing right). So far, so good. But he also says that we require transcendence: some way of getting beyond our finite limitations. He is not alone. Many people insist that, if we are confined to just this life and this world, we do not have enough to provide life with meaning. Sophia's atheist, materialist version of meaning is just too thin a gruel for us to survive on.

I'm just not convinced that the human 'yearning for transcendence', as Cottingham puts it, is really universal and basic. I know plenty of people who don't feel it. But even if they do, the fact that you desire something does not show that that thing must exist. If an honest look at the world leads us to conclude we are stuck in our mortal bodies for a finite time in a physical world, no amount of yearning for something else is going to make it otherwise. Arguing that we cannot do without transcendence is the intellectual equivalent of thumping a fist on a table and insisting, 'It must be so!'

I'm also not convinced that this modest account of life's meaning is such thin gruel after all. Rather, our expectations of what we need to nourish ourselves are often just wrong. People who demand more than this world has to offer are like people who believe that eating well requires elaborate recipes and rich sauces. Faced with porridge or a simple pasta, they insist that this isn't enough. But, in fact, in the long run, their fancy diet is much less nutritious and no more delicious than the plainer fare provided by simple cooking from fresh ingredients.

PAUSE AND REMEMBER
ALFRED WAINWRIGHT

FELLWALKER, GUIDE BOOK AUTHOR
AND ILLUSTRATOR
WHO LOVED THIS VALLEY.

LIFT YOUR EYES TO HAYSTACKS
HIS FAVOURITE PLACE.

1907 - 1991

▲ Life after death need not be our only hope.

▶ Back to the start

Albert Camus famously compared life to the myth of Sisyphus, condemned by the gods to roll a huge rock up a hill, only for it to roll down to the bottom again, where he had to start the pushing all over again. This futile process went on forever, but Sisyphus, said Camus, can be happy by embracing his fate, and we too can be happy by accepting that our fate is, in a sense, absurd too. Before a chance encounter of sperm and egg, we were nothing. We are born, we live, we strive to make our lives meaningful and then one day, our heart stops and we are no more again. We can kick and scream if we like, protesting at the 'meaninglessness' of it all, or we can get on with it and, if not be happy, at least find positive reasons to live.

What Camus didn't point out is that philosophy is something of a Sisyphean task as well. In this book, I have portrayed it as starting with questions that directly relate to the meaning or purpose and life, which leads to ever more abstract and general issues, which then feed back to inform our understanding of who we were and how we should live. This is a circle, however, without any real beginning or end. It can be picked up at any point: some come to philosophy through logical or epistemology, others politics or aesthetics. But anyone who, having started, really thinks hard and deeply will find themselves being drawn both back and forth from the more general to their more specific concerns.

However, unlike Sisyphus, each time we find ourselves at the bottom of the hill again, we find that things have changed. The rock and hill no longer look the same and we have learned more about how to push the rock and why we should bother. The rock is still where it was but we have made progress on ourselves, internally. That is why philosophy is particularly rewarding: no matter how many times you come back to the most basic questions and canonical texts, there is something new to learn. As Peter Strawson wrote, 'There is no shallow end to the philosophical pool.'

At least, that is how it should be. But it is possible to live and think like Sisyphus, merely repeating without ever making progress. In thought and in life, there is always the risk of mere repetition. I think it matters to keep thinking, to keep learning, to keep progressing in some way. We can find meaning in life in a huge variety of ways, and I do not deny that some find it by simply doing what they love, again and again. But life is richer when it contains more days that could not be replaced by any other without any noticeable effect. I think we are all aware of the kind of existential shock we get when we realize a long period of time has passed and we have 'done nothing'. Of course, we have not done nothing at all – it is often because we have been busy that time seems to have vanished. What we mean is that we have done nothing other than what we normally do. Each day has been too much like any other. We have been caught in stasis but time has marched on, taking with it more of the precious hours of which we have so few.

Making the most of life is not just about throwing ourselves into a frantic whirl of experiences. Inner activity is what really keeps us most alive, because it is through having minds, thoughts and ideas that we exist as human persons and not just animals. So we must keep thinking. Philosophy is one way to do that, and one of the most demanding as well as most rewarding. No introduction to philosophy can contain all that matters about it, but it can, I hope, show where all that matters about it is to be found: in the doing of philosophy as a project without end.

This 100 ideas section gives ways you can explore the subject in more depth. It's much more than just the usual reading list.

100 IDEAS

5 sites of philosophical pilgrimage

1   Athens. There are surprisingly few sites with specific links to philosophy in the city where it all first flowered, but you can see the underwhelming location of Plato's Academy, a cave which is said to be Socrates' prison cell but almost certainly is not, and the agora where he questioned all and sundry so closely.

2   Paris. Have coffee in Les Deux Magots, favourite left-bank haunt of existentialists such as Jean-Paul Sartre and Simone de Beauvoir, before going to visit their joint grave at the Cimetière du Montparnasse and worshipping reason at the secular temple that is the Pantheon.

3   **Wittgenstein's dwellings**. Choose between his simple rural hut in Skjolden, Norway, and the Haus Wittgenstein that he designed in Vienna.

4   **Berlin**. Pay your respects at the graves of Hegel and Fichte at the Dorotheenstädtischer Friedhof Cemetery and sit at Hegel's desk in Room 3103 of Humbolt University, where Wittgenstein also taught and from where Marx graduated.

5   **Edinburgh**. Tip your hat to the statue of Hume on the Royal Mile and to his mausoleum in Old Calton Burial Ground, and visit Riddle's Court, where he lived from 1751.

10 quotes

6   'It is the mark of an educated man to look for precision in each class of things just so far as the nature of the subject admits.' Aristotle (384–322 BCE)

7   'Say to yourself in the early morning: I shall meet today inquisitive, ungrateful, violent, treacherous, envious, uncharitable men. All these things have come upon them through ignorance of real good and ill.' Marcus Aurelius (121–180)

8   'No man can have a peaceful life who thinks too much about lengthening it.' Seneca (c. 4 BCE to 65 AD)

9   'Nothing is so firmly believed as that which least is known.' Michel de Montaigne (1533–1592)

10 'He that uses his words loosely and unsteadily will either not be minded or not understood.' John Locke (1632–1704)

11 'We have first raised a dust and then complain we cannot see.' George Berkeley (1685–1753)

12 'Be a philosopher but, amid all your philosophy, be still a man.' David Hume (1711–1776)

13 'The happiest is he who suffers least; the most miserable is he who enjoys least.' Jean-Jacques Rousseau (1712–1778)

14 'Morality is not properly the doctrine of how we should make ourselves happy, but how we should become worthy of happiness.' Immanuel Kant (1724–1804)

15 'The point of philosophy is to start with something so simple as not to seem worth stating, and to end with something so paradoxical that no one will believe it.' Bertrand Russell (1872–1970)

5 philosophical films

16 **Rashomon** (directed by Akira Kurosawa, 1950)

17 **Life of Brian** (directed by Terry Jones, 1979)

18 **Crimes and Misdemeanors** (directed by Woody Allen, 1989)

19 **Fargo** (directed by Joel and Ethan Coen, 1996)

20 **Memento** (directed by Christopher Nolan, 2000)

5 philosophical plays

21 **Dangerous Corner** by J B Priestley (1932)

22 **Huis Clos [No Exit]** by Jean-Paul Sartre (1944)

23 **A Man for All Seasons** by Robert Bolt (1960)

24 **Arcadia** by Tom Stoppard (1993)

25 **Copenhagen** by Michael Frayn (1998)

5 novels of ideas

26 **Candide** by Voltaire (1759)

27 **The Brothers Karamazov** by Fyodor Dostoyevsky (1879–1880)

28 **L'Étranger [The Outsider]** by Albert Camus (1942)

29 **The Hitchhiker's Guide to the Galaxy** by Douglas Adams (1979)

30 **The Unbearable Lightness of Being** by Milan Kundera (1984)

5 great paintings of philosophers

31 **David Hume by Allan Ramsay** (1766), Scottish National Portrait Gallery, Edinburgh

32 **Rousseau by Allan Ramsay** (1766), Scottish National Portrait Gallery, Edinburgh

33 **School of Athens by Raphael** (1510–1511), The Apostolic Palace, The Vatican

34 **Death of Socrates by Jacques-Louis David** (1787), Metropolitan Museum of Art, New York

35 **Friedrich Nietzsche by Edvard Munch** (1906), Munch Museum, Oslo

5 top websites

36 **Internet Encyclopedia of Philosophy** (www.iep.utm.edu)

37 **Stanford Encyclopedia of Philosophy** (http://plato.stanford.edu)

38 EpistemeLinks (www.epistemelinks.com)

39 The Philosophers' Magazine (www.thephilosophers-magazine.com)

40 David Chalmers (http://consc.net/chalmers)

5 podcasts

41 Philosophy Bites (Nigel Warburton and David Edmonds, www.philosophybites.com)

42 In Our Time Philosophy Archive (BBC, www.bbc.co.uk/podcasts/series/iot)

43 History of philosophy (Peter Adamson, www.kcl.ac.uk/ikings/index.php?id=487)

44 Microphilosophy (Julian Baggini, www.microphilosophy.net)

45 The Philosopher's Zone (Australian Broadcasting Corporation, www.abc.net.au/radionational/programs/philosopherszone/)

10 public philosophers worth listening to

46 Simon Blackburn

47 Daniel Dennett

48 Jürgen Habermas

49 Martha Nussbaum

50 Onora O'Neill

51 Michael Sandel

52 Amartya Sen

53 Peter Singer

54 Mary Warnock

55 Slavoj Žižek

10 readable (but not always easy) classics

56 Plato, *The Republic* (c. 380–360 BCE)

57 Aristotle, *Nicomachean Ethics* (c. 350 BCE)

58 René Descartes, *Meditations on First Philosophy* (1641)

59 David Hume, *Dialogues Concerning Natural Religion* (1779)

60 Søren Kierkegaard, *Fear and Trembling* (1843)

61 John Stuart Mill, *On Liberty* (1869)

62 Jean-Paul Sartre, *Existentialism and Humanism* (1946)

63 A J Ayer, *Language, Truth and Logic* (1936)

64 Ludwig Wittgenstein, *Philosophical Investigations* (1953)

65 Gilbert Ryle, *The Concept of Mind* (1949)

10 principles

66 The Mean (Aristotle). Virtues should be understood not as opposites of vices but as lying between two opposite extremes of vice. So generosity lies between meanness and profligacy, courage between cowardice and rashness, and so on.

67 Just War (Thomas Aquinas). It is justified to go to war only if it is the last resort, the action is proportionate, there is a good chance of success and the warring party has legitimate authority and the right intentions. Once in war, non-combatants should be respected and all action should be kept proportionate.

68 Occam's Razor (William of Occam). Entities should not be multiplied beyond necessity. In other words, all other things being equal (a vital caveat), simpler explanations are preferable to more complicated ones.

69 The Principle of Sufficient Reason (Gottfried Leibniz). 'Nothing is without a reason for why it is rather than is not.'

70 The Principle of Evidence (David Hume). 'A wise man proportions his belief to the evidence' and 'a weaker evidence can never destroy a stronger'.

71 'Ought' implies 'can' (Immanuel Kant). You cannot say someone ought to do something unless it is possible that he or she can do so.

72 The Harm Principle (John Stuart Mill). 'The sole end for which mankind are warranted, individually or collectively, in interfering with the liberty of action of any of their number, is self-protection. That the only purpose for which power can be rightfully exercised over any member of a civilized community, against his will, is to prevent harm to others. His own good, either physical or moral, is not sufficient warrant.'

73 The Falsification Principle (Karl Popper). For a claim to be scientific it must be possible that it is testable in such a way that failure to pass the test would show that it is wrong.

74 The Principle of Charity (Donald Davidson). When critiquing the claims of others, interpret them so as to make them as reasonable as possible.

75 The Difference Principle (John Rawls). Increases in inequality are permissible only if they benefit the worst-off members of society.

10 common fallacies

76 The gambler's fallacy. Thinking that the probability of an event occurring changes depending on what has happened before, even though prior events have no causal role in the event. For example, believing that if you toss a coin and it comes up heads, it is more likely to come up tails next time.

77 Post hoc fallacy. Falsely assuming that what happened before something caused it. For example, a person might touch a lucky charm and then win the lottery, and assume that it was because they touched the charm that they won. Maybe, but maybe not. . .

78 Affirming the consequent. If it's Tuesday, the shop will be open. The shop is open. Therefore it's Tuesday. No: the shops might also open on other days. This form of argument (If x then y; y, therefore x) is, however, often seductive. For example, you have some cheese and think, 'If I'm lactose intolerant, then I'll get a stomach ache'. You get a stomach ache and conclude that you are lactose intolerant. But there might have been another cause for the pain.

79 Straw man fallacy. Dismissing a position by criticizing no more than a weak or distorted version of it.

80 Ad hominem. Dismissing an argument on the basis of criticisms of the person making it, rather than on its own merits.

81 **Democratic fallacy**. Arguing that something is right or true because most people think it is.

82 **Genetic fallacy**. Confusing the origins of an idea with what justifies it. For example, dismissing the science behind the health risks of tobacco because Nazi doctors were the first to investigate them.

83 **Argument from authority**. Arguing that something is true purely on the basis that someone you hold to be the authority says it is. Tricky, because we all have to defer to experts to some extent.

84 **No true Scotsman move**. Antony Flew told the story of a man who claimed that no Scotsman could commit the heinous crime reported in the news. When it transpired that a Scotsman had done just that, he said that no true Scotsman would do such a thing. Likewise, we can maintain the illusion that any group we think is great against counter-evidence by claiming that those who fall short aren't true members of the group.

85 **Begging the question**. Assuming precisely what is in question. For instance, to ask how someone stayed alive for a year subsisting solely on fresh air, you assume that they did in fact do so.

5 good introductions

86 **Philosophy: Key Texts** and **Philosophy: Key Themes** (second editions) by Julian Baggini and Gareth Southwell (Palgrave Macmillan)

87 **Think** by Simon Blackburn (Oxford University Press)

88 **Philosophy: A Very Short Introduction** by Edward Craig (Oxford University Press)

89 **The Problems of Philosophy** by Bertrand Russell (Oxford University Press)

90 **Philosophy: The Classics** edited by Nigel Warburton (Routledge)

5 best philosophical one-liners

91 J L Austin gave a lecture in which he claimed that although there were languages where a double negative implied a positive, there was none in which a double positive indicated a negative. To which Sydney Morgenbesser replied dismissively, 'Yeah, yeah'.

92 Wittgenstein famously concluded his *Tractatus Logico-Philosophicus* with the line, 'What we cannot speak about we must pass over in silence.' Frank Ramsey wrote in reply, 'But what we can't say, we can't say, and we can't whistle it either.'

93 'It is my personal opinion that Mr Wittgenstein's thesis is a work of genius; but, be that as it may, it is certainly well up to the standard required for the Cambridge degree of Doctor of Philosophy.' G E Moore is supposed to have said this in his examiner's report, although it seems the original version might be the less funny 'I myself consider that this is a work of genius; but, even if I am completely mistaken and it is nothing of the sort, it is well above the standard required for the PhD degree.'

94 In 1987 in New York, the then 77-year-old A J Ayer intervened to stop the boxer Mike Tyson harassing the model Naomi Campbell. As reported in Ben Rogers's biography of Ayer, Tyson said, 'Do you know who the fuck I am? I'm the heavyweight champion of the world.' Ayer replied, 'And I am the former Wykeham Professor of Logic. We are both pre-eminent in our field. I suggest that we talk about this like rational men.' It worked.

95 'I refute Berkeley thus.' This is actually the worst one-liner in the history of philosophy. Dr Johnson apparently said this kicking a stone, claiming that it disproved Berkeley's theories that there was no matter, only ideas. But Berkeley did not think that this meant ideas appeared any less concrete to us than they do, so Johnson's retort misses the point.

5 most intractable philosophical questions of all time

96 How does science work?

97 Why should we be moral?

98 How do people with different values live together?

99 How is consciousness possible?

100 Do we have free will and, if so, what is it?

Index

abstraction
  principles 18–19
  questions 4, 6–8, 15–16, 49–53, 125–126, 133
aesthetics 5, 91, 94–5, 96, 97, 128, 133
Appiah, Kwame Anthony 113
Arab Spring 101
Aristotle 16–19, 41, 65, 70, 81, 83, 101–104
  ethics, morality and 112, 113, 115
  life, meaning of 125, 127, 128, 129
art
  non-art and 91–3
  value of 93–7
asking 'why?' 3–5
Ayer, A.J. 17

Bacon, Francis 58–61, 62
Bakunin, Mikhail 104–5
Bearsley, Monroe 95
Bell, Clive 94
Bentham, Jeremy 94
Berkeley, Bishop George 18, 30–8
Boyle, Robert 69
Buddha 84, 85

Camus, Albert 132–143
causal connections 44–6, 46–9
Cebes 82–3
Chisholm, Roderick 36
Christianity 76, 82, 109, 112
Coady, C.A.J. 121
Coomaraswamy, Ananda 94
cosmology 71–83
Cottingham, John 130–31

Danto, Arthur C. 93
Descartes, René 18

Dewey, John 18, 96
duty, deontology and 116–118, 128

essence, search for 81–4
ethics 111–136
  morality and 113–118
experimental philosophy 69

fallacies 142–3
falsifiability 61–63
fashion 93
Feyerabend, Paul 65
films 137
free will 49–53
Frege, Gottlob 33

Galileo 77
Glaucon 82
goodness (and doing good) 111–112, 112–14
government, forms of 101–104
growth of philosophy 5–8

Hawking, Stephen 41–42
Hobbes, Thomas 106–108
Hood, Bruce 87
Hooke, Robert 69
Hsun Tzu 96
Hume, David 18, 47, 85–6, 115–118, 120, 127, 129
Hutcheson, Francis 115–116

induction 57-61
intractable questions 145
introductory texts 143-4

James, William 18

Kant, Immanuel 31, 93–4, 120, 128
knowledge, meaning of 11, 19–23
Kuhn, Thomas 63–65

language 27, 32–38
Leibniz, Gottfried Wilhelm 18
life, meaning of 125–31
Locke, John 18, 30, 69

metaphysics 41–43, 57
method 63–65
Metzinger, Thomas 87
moral philosophy 113, 121–22

natural science, philosophy and 69–71
necessary connections 46–9
neuroscience 84, 87
Nicene Creed 76
novels of ideas 138

one-liners 144–5

paintings 138
Pascal's Wager 73
Peirce, Charles Sanders 18
perception 27–32, 38
philosophical anthropology 5–8
philosophical one-liners 144–5
philosophical pilgrimage, sites for 136–7
Picasso, Pablo 95
Plato 13–16, 29, 37, 81–2, 83, 101–4, 25
   ethics, morality and 112, 113, 115
plays 137
podcasts 139
Pol Pot 102
politics 101–4
Popper, Karl 61–63, 5

principles 140–42
public philosophers 139–40
Pythagoras 87

quantum theory 51, 57, 66–7
quotations 136–7

readable classics 140
reflection 5–8
religion
   persistence of 74–77
   philosophy of 71–74, 74–77
Rousseau, Jean-Jacques 106–108
Royal Society, foundation of 69
Russell, Bertrand 18
Ryle, Gilbert 34–5

Sartre, Jean-Paul 84
Schiller, Friedrich von 96
Schopenhauer, Arthur 96
science (and scientific research), nature of 41–2, 64–5
self
   five khandhas of 84–5
   self-awareness 81, 84–87
Shakespeare, William 113–114
Siddhārtha Gautama 84
Sistine Chapel 95
Sisyphus 132–3
Smith, Adam 115–116
Socrates 19, 81–2, 81–7, 83, 136
Spinoza, Baruch 18
state
   justification for 104–8
   politics and 104–9105
Strawson, Peter 133

Tolstoy, Leo 95–6
truth, meaning of 11, 19–23

universe 43–46
utilitarianism 121

websites 138–9
Wilkins, John 69

Wimsatt, W.K. 95
Wittgenstein, Ludwig von 32,
    34, 35, 75, 92
Wolpert, Lewis 41–50
wonder 75, 125–128
Wren, Christopher 69

ALL THAT MATTERS: PHILOSOPHY